Basketball
and the
Rio Grande
College Legend

By Newt Oliver
with
Dr. Danny Fulks

Copyright 1995
Price $6.95
FIRST EDITION

Introduction

The early 1950s were easy times in the United States. Jobs were readily available. You could go up north to a big city and pull down $100 a week. Many did. The nation was segregated between blacks and whites. Down in Montgomery, Alabama, Rosa Parks quietly moved to the back of the bus on her way to work and back. College students danced under the stars to Perry Como and Frank Sinatra. Elvis Presley, his hair shining with Rose Oil hair tonic, was a student at Humes High School in Memphis. The McDonald Brothers sold fifteen-cent hamburgers in California. Ray Kroc, who later bought them out, was selling paper cups. Suburbs were springing up around the cities where new houses started at $11,500. Money was cheap and easy to borrow. Kemings Wilson of Memphis griped about paying an extra $2 for each child when the family stayed in motels. Within a few years, he would put Holiday Inns at thousands of exits along the interstates. Children stayed free. Milton Berle, dressed in drag, came in Tuesday nights to every home that had a television set. Black and white. Marlon Brando, James Dean, and Marilyn Monroe—sullen, sultry, sexy—replaced Clark Gable and John Wayne as screen idols. Alfred Kinsey hadn't published the reports on human sexual behavior. The Pill hadn't been perfected. Hugh Hefner had a new magazine in his head, Playboy. But it hadn't hit the newsstands yet. There were only about 400 Volkswagen Beetles around. American car designers stuck with chrome and fins, and kept the gas guzzlers coming. Mikey Spillane's hero, Mike Hammer, was the literary rage. The Korean War was winding down.

Rio Grande, a placid little village in southeastern Ohio, was as quiet as it ever was. Maybe quieter. It was "dry" —

always was. The most raucous place in town was Frank Denny's Restaurant north of State Route 35. Hank Williams was dead. His hit song, *I'll Never Get Out of This World Alive*, blasted from giant speakers in the Rock-Ola juke box. A pin-ball machine, with flashing lights blinking around shapely girls in swim suits, made the familiar sounds of steel balls jumping out of pop-up holes. Semi-trailers moved through on their way north. People went to bed early. On Sundays, almost everyone in town made their way to the Calvary Baptist Church to hear a sermon and sing the old hymns.

There was a college in the village. Since 1876, Rio Grande had turned out teachers and preachers. It was a small college supported by the American Baptist Association. Manners and morals were firm. No drinking, no smoking, no sex. Well, not much. And those who indulged, at least, felt guilty. Students were to keep their minds clear and pure by attending a re-quired chapel service each week, going to vespers in the Dugout, and reading Cicero. Sports were also offered to men and women. Intramural games of tennis, soccer, softball, and track were played. Men's basketball was introduced in 1916. In 1920 six players dressed. During World War II, when stu-dent enrollment dropped to forty-four, basketball barely sur-vived. After the war, a series of coaches attempted to keep the sport alive. But when Rio Grande College made the newspa-pers, it was more likely to be a story about Founder's Day when students and faculty solemnly marched to a graveyard near the campus to strew flowers on the graves of its dead leaders than about its athletic feats. Bloo-o-ey, Bow, Wow,—Choo-o-ey, Chow, Chow—Hoo-o-ray, Pow-w,—Rio Grande, went the chant. Few were there to hear it. But in the sweaty high school gyms of the region new chants were being re-hearsed. Unaware of unfolding events, younger girls with harder legs and shorter skirts that twirled over bright satin tights, prepared for a fling that would see a select few of them lead cheers for the Rio Grande College Redmen in front of 13,000 cheering sports fans at New York City's Madison Square Garden.

The United States was ready for a hero. Coming here to Rio Grande College, a school nobody outside of the region had ever heard of, was a country boy from Wellsville, Ohio, named Clarence "Bevo" Francis. He was brought there by an equally unknown coach from Byesville, Ohio, named Newt Oliver. The promise of money to support this combination and their players was made by Don Allen, a native of Rio Grande and was the world's largest Chevrolet dealer. This is Newt Oliver's story.

Newt Oliver

Newt Oliver is a man who made life a challenge to everything he approached. He has been a truck driver, college professor, high school teacher, coal miner, steel mill laborer, farmer, politician, high school and college basketball coach, professional basketball coach, businessman, college trustee, conservationist, and public relations director for Abe Saperstein's Harlem Globetrotters.

In 1954, Saperstein called Newt Oliver the greatest college basketball promoter who ever lived. He took Rio Grande College from oblivion to national and international fame. Never before, nor since, has a college basketball team captured the imagination of the country as the Rio Grande College Redmen of 1952-54.

There are many stories told and recorded about basketball history. None is as colorful and exciting as the legendary Rio Grande College team, its offensive machine, and Bevo Francis, the greatest scorer in the history of college basketball. The team's renown and its legendary scorer are forever enshrined in the record books. For forty-one years, this team has dominated the conversations about teams who live on in the legendary world of sports. As a player and an individual scorer, Bevo Francis has a singular place among America's great basketball players.

This Redmen team captured the imagination of America's sports fans with a style of play never before seen in the great arenas of this country. Hundreds of thousands of people came down the two-lane blacktops on game nights to see them in action. Even people who were not sports fanatics lined up at the ticket booths. Fans crowded around the Redmen bench and leaned forward in their seats to catch a glimpse of the 6' 9" Francis, a tall shooter in the days when shorter players dominated the game. And this story happened in times when special diets, athletic trainers, weight rooms, psychologists, shoe contracts, and publicity agents were unknown in college sports.

The story that follows will separate fact from fiction. This is Newt Oliver's account. It was he who brought the team and the resources together. He was a colorful coach in a time when other college coaches were bland. He coached to win. But he also coached to entertain the crowds and the media. As you read this story, you will hear in your mind the coach's shouts to "feed Bevo." You will smell the sweat of the players and fans and the popcorn. You will feel the cold from the frosted windows in large auditoriums on cold winter nights. You will see Bevo Francis bring the score on the lighted boards that look down on the crowd go up, up, up. Eighty, eighty-five, ninety-five, one hundred and thirteen. You will hear the screams and yells as the story unfolds.

BASKETBALL AND THE RIO GRANDE LEGEND— THE FIRST YEAR

It was the summer of 1952. I was finishing up my work for a Master of Science Degree in Public Health and Physical Education at the University of Wyoming in Laramie. It was a relaxing time there on the campus far away from the confines of Wellsville, Ohio, where I was coaching at a local High School. No pushy parents of mediocre players around. No irate school board members. No petty bureaucratic clerks. On weekends, my wife, Maxine, and I would pack a picnic basket and head out to the Medicine Bow National Park taking in the great vistas that contrasted with central Ohio's flat plains. This was high country. The land of great American cowboys and the cattle drives of the nineteenth century. The land of the

The University of Wyoming

The Graduate School

Know all men by these presents, That

John Newton Oliver

having completed the appropriate Course of Study prescribed by the Graduate Faculty, and having fulfilled all other requirements, is therefore granted the degree of

Master of Science in Physical Education

In Testimony Whereof, this Diploma has been granted, attested with the Seal of the University and with the Signatures of its duly authorized officers at Laramie, Wyoming, this 15th day of August, in the year of our Lord nineteen hundred and fifty-two.

PRESIDENT OF THE BOARD OF TRUSTEES

PRESIDENT OF THE UNIVERSITY

SECRETARY OF THE BOARD OF TRUSTEES

DEAN

1

friendly Arapaho Indians, many of whom still walked the streets of Laramie. Rodeo country. Hank Thompson's song, *Honky Tonk Angels*, blasted from every jukebox. One night, we were at our apartment. I was working on a term paper for one of my classes. The phone rang.

President Charles Davis of Rio Grande College was on the phone. Would I be interested in the job of head basketball coach there, he wanted to know. I asked for some time to think about it. Talk it over with Maxine. He gave me three days. We talked. Maxine urged me to take it. She would be only a few miles from her home. This was a date with destiny that would forever change my life. Over the next two years we lived a basketball story so fascinating that it became legendary in scope and historic in significance. Appalachian writer, Dr. Danny Fulks, told the story in the Ohio Historical Society's *Timeline* magazine, February-March, 1992. The story was given seventeen pages, and, in my estimation, it was the best researched and complete story ever written about the team and Bevo. It reads like fiction. But it was the greatest true basketball story that has happened since the game was originated in the cold of December at Springfield, Massachusetts in 1891. I lived it. But I thought it was a dream in December 1953 when the team and fans carried me off the floor of the Reynolds Coliseum in Raleigh, North Carolina, after we defeated Wake Forest 67 to 65. Most of the people in the auditorium that night had never heard of Rio Grande College.

This great Redmen team began with a plan I formulated during the 1947-48 season when I was a basketball player at Rio Grande. Even at that young age, I wondered if it would be possible for this small school to play major college teams across the United States. Would an aggressive coach, who saw no limits to what his team could do, practice and play in a gymnasium that seated 150 people? Could a team with one worn-out basketball eventually play in the major basketball arenas of the United States? Could this little college get more national recognition than any college basketball team in the sport's history? I had the dream.

2

Byesville, Ohio, is a village in Guernsey County about halfway between Columbus and Wheeling, West Virginia. It lies just south of the old National Road that took thousands of settlers west in the nineteenth century. Today, interstate highways 70 and 77 intersect at nearby Cambridge. There were many hungry, unemployed people in Byesville in the early 1930s, but the residents there were people of strong spirit and character. When the Byesville High School basketball team, the Falcons, took to the hardwood on Friday nights, the village united behind them. This team gave them hope and helped them forget the bitter hard times. I will never forget seeing the enthusiasm displayed by these fans as they ran wild across the floor after a close victory over an opponent. However, coaches there were often prone to political pressures. A coach did not make big money. But the $1,200 a year they made enabled them to live well in a place where most men were lucky to take home $300 a year in wages. And many had no job at all. So those young men whose fathers were influential in the community—lawyers, doctors, school board members—were often played in basketball games even if their talents were limited. Better players from poor families often sat on the bench. This was typical in close knit, poor communities. On the up side, it was seen as taking care of one's own. On the down side, it taught the less fortunate a bitter lesson about life. Byesville was a sports village, but the money to run a first-class program was not there.

During my time on the floor in junior high and high school, I became used to the reality that the more influential your family was, and the more the coach liked you, the more minutes you spent in the game. I knew then that if I ever became a high school basketball coach, my players' personalities and their social status would have nothing to do with their playing time. I would let nothing but ability and willingness to play hard dictate my decisions. We played a schedule that consisted of other high schools with colorful names: Pleasant City, Trail Run, Buffalo, Cumberland, Old Washington, Caldwell and Bell Valley. The rivalry was intense. I played for two coaches in high school, neither of whom ever played on a competitive

Byesville High School 1941-42 basketball team, Byesville, Ohio. Number 12, Newt Oliver, five years later at Rio Grande College led the nation in scoring with 725 points. Cliff Wilson, shown holding the ball, later was a star center at Rio Grande. The Byesville team was coached by Howard Thomas.

level. They had little feel for the game, how it should be played and coached. The nature of the game was, however, changing. The slow, deliberate game with the two-hand set shot was giving way to the one-hand jump shot and, at times, a run-and-gun approach. One of my coaches called the one-hand jump shot a circus shot, and if you used this type of shot, you did not play. We were playing 1920s' style ball into the 1940s. Even though Byesville played against teams that were coached in an up-tempo style that was sweeping the country, Byesville coaches held back.

During my senior year in high school, the United States entered World War II. I graduated in 1942 and enrolled that fall at Kent State University. It was a cold school in a cold town in a place where winters were extremely rugged. Dissatisfied there, I enlisted in the United States Coast Guard. I played three years of service basketball. As those years passed, I matured both physically and mentally. After the war, I returned to Byesville where I played basketball in a variety of unstructured leagues while looking for a college that might suit my style and personality. I had decided to become a high school coach.

In October, 1945, I drove out one day to watch a football game between the Fletcher Army Hospital of Cambridge, Ohio, and Rio Grande College. I had never heard of Rio Grande, but I liked what I saw that day. Here was a group of young men who had ridden up in an old school bus. They had only a handful of players and their uniforms were scruffy, but they gave the game everything they had even in defeat. The next day I wrote to the registrar at Rio Grande asking for a catalog and an enrollment application.

Basketball would become Rio Grande's route to fame. Football never had a chance. Its football teams during the 1940s had the longest losing streak among colleges in the United States. This dubious distinction was reported in newspapers nationwide. Perhaps this should not be too surprising. The school's total enrollment dropped as low as forty-four, and most men fit to play any kind of ball were in Uncle Sam's

Army. In September 1944 the losing streak was broken. With game uniforms that did not match and players from all walks of life—some of whom were not even enrolled in school—they won a convincing game against Muskingum College of New Concord, Ohio. In basketball that year Rio Grande made history by losing to Morehead State in Kentucky. The score was 81-15, the most lopsided game in the annals of college basketball. Still the preachers assembled for weekly prayers at the College Christian Association's home in the Dugout and the few students there persevered on to get their degrees.

I drove down to Rio Grande for the first time in 1945. The war was over, things were looking up, Harry Truman was president, and Clark Gable had returned to star in a new flick with Greer Garson. I looked the program over, talked with the basketball coach, and chatted with a few students hanging around the Allen House. Frank Allen, Don's father, ran a college rooming house that was home to a dozen or more men, most of whom were seasoned war veterans going to school on the GI Bill. In spite of Allen's dignified manner and frugality, games of five-card stud were in progress around the clock. The next day, I attended one of the coach's practice sessions. He counted off the players into two teams and had them scrimmage for an hour with no referee and no individual instruction. It was alley basketball on a refined level. Nothing was defined. Discouraged, I went back to the Allen House and began packing my bags to head home to Byesville. But I decided to give it one more try. The second practice was different. The coach had on a different outfit. He sat in a different seat in the Hog Pen, a name appropriately given to Community Hall. The practice was the same. No instructions. Another hour of knock down, drag out alley basketball. This time I threw my stuff in my 1933 Ford Roadster and, telling no one, headed home. This was a three-hour drive north on two-lane blacktop, most of the time with double yellow lines in the center. You might follow a semi-trailer for a half-an-hour before having a chance to pass. The car's windshield wipers slapped against large, wet snow flakes. Burma-Shave signs, Mail Pouch barns, Camel cigarette billboards, and Perry

Como's voice on the radio kept me company. But Christmas was coming, and it would be good to get home. Christmas day was my twenty-second birthday.

Back in Byesville, I played on the village's American Legion basketball team at night and hunted rabbits by day. We ate enough rabbit dinners that winter to last any normal family a lifetime. In the summer of 1946, my father gave me two options: either go farther north to Canton and get my old job back that I had in 1942 at the Hercules Motor Corporation or go to college. I knew that if I ever went back to a factory job, basketball and my dreams of becoming a college player and coach would forever vanish.

So in September 1946, I again made my way to Rio Grande. I enrolled as a freshman in secondary education. If I could complete this program, a job coaching basketball in high school should be mine for the taking. We played seventeen games that season, winning only four. For most of the season, I led the state of Ohio in college scoring. I could have been number one, but the coach's philosophy was that he did not want any player to excel over the others no matter how much ability he had. At age twenty-three, I found that I was often playing with and against younger kids just out of high school. I discovered that experience and maturity were valuable assets. It was as though I had four years of varsity experience. During the 1946 football season, the college did have its most successful athletic year in history. It won five and lost two. This team, comprised mainly of rugged World War II veterans, also showed the advantages that mentally and physically fit players could bring to a team. As a sophomore player in 1947-48, my place on the basketball team became secure. I scored 725 points that season, the top scorer in the United States, and I set an all-time national record for free throws with 291. Honors that season included honorable mention on an All-American team picked by officials from the Converse Company. The players on that team included men from Division One. I also made the first team selection of the All-Midwest team which was comprised of several states. I knew then that if I ever got

1947-48 Rio Grande College Basketball Team. The most unsual basketball team in America as four of the starting five players were from Byesville, Ohio, which was Newt Oliver's home town
Left to Right: Newt Oliver, Dave Heady, Cliff Wilson, Ike Murnahan, Ted McHenry. (Murnahan was the outsider from Ironton, Ohio.)

a chance to coach at Rio Grande, I had a plan to bring national acclaim to the college.

In my senior year at Rio Grande, a new coach was hired. Bob Stoneburner, who had coached during my second year, moved on to another school. My third and last season, Joe Gibson of Pennsylvania was hired. By attending school both winters and summers, I completed the requirements for a Bachelor of Science Degree in three years. Each of my three years was played under different coaches. In the summer of 1948, Cam Henderson, the famous coach at Marshall College, offered me a free ride if I would transfer there and play my senior year with the Thundering Herd. When I talked this over with Don Allen, he told me he would give me a new Chevrolet if I stayed at Rio Grande. He sent the car and I stayed. During my playing career, I played for eighteen coaches. I learned something positive from each of them. I dismissed from my memory what I felt were many goofy approaches.

In the spring of 1949, degree in hand, I found that Upper Sandusky, Ohio, needed a coach. Charles Davis was superintendent of schools in Upper Sandusky. This was flat country. Pretty much in the middle of nowhere. Upper Sandusky is located about one hour north of Columbus on State Route 23. It is about halfway between Findlay and Marion, equally obscure cities. Were it not for President Warren G. Harding's home in Marion, few people would have ever heard of any of the three cities. It was far from my idea of a romantic place to start my coaching career. But it was a job. And it turned out well. Many local fans still believe that my first year there produced the best team the school ever had. The season was not long under way until my resolve to play talent, and talent only, was tested. A father of one of the players walked up to me one night during half time of a game. He asked me why his son wasn't playing. I told him it was because he wasn't good enough. This man had influence in the community and he felt his son should be in the game regardless of his ability. He threatened to circulate a petition to get me fired if his son didn't get more time on the hardwood. I told him that was fine

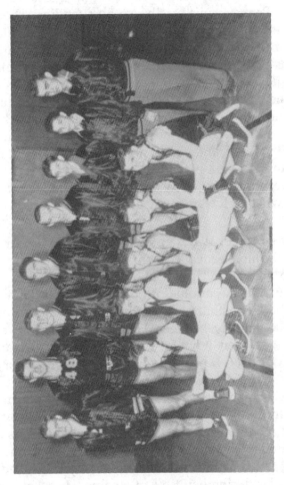

Coach Newt Oliver's first team 1949-50, the Ram's of Upper Sandusky, Ohio.
Kneeling—Bob Long, Franklin Leightey, Earl Messmer, Roy Moses, Tom Kotterman.
Standing—Jim Mason, Ronnie Koehler, Tom Kimmel, Jerry Wall, Maurice Carpenter,
Managers; Jim Shaffer, Dick Corbin, Allen Pagnard.

with me, but the boy won't be in the lineup until he was good enough to help us win. The boy later quit the team. But the word was out. Newt Oliver was not going to succumb to the downtown coaches, influential parents, and pushy school board members. The solid citizens of Upper Sandusky backed me all the way.

I spent one more year at Upper Sandusky, then resigned to take the basketball coaching job at Wellsville in Columbiana County. As Upper Sandusky is located on a flat plain, Wellsville is in a land of rugged terrain. The Ohio River curves by on its murky way to the Gulf of Mexico. The surrounding hills are steep, covered with strong growths of hardwood timber. Wellsville has the dubious honor of being the town where Pretty Boy Floyd was shot and killed during the great outlaw escapades of the 1930s. My belief has always been that a high school coach should own a car, a few personal items, a couple of suits, and his pride. So when the going gets tough, he will be ready to move on to a new school. The job at

As a high school player, Bevo Francis stood head and shoulders above his teammates, shown here with Ron Weekly in the Wellsville High School gym, during the 1951-52 season.

Wellsville was the great turning point in my life for it was there that I met Bevo Francis and we, for the next few exciting years, would be inseparable. Like Upper Sandusky, the people of Wellsville loved their athletic teams.

Wellsville had two brickyards that provided jobs for many laborers. Smoke from the kilns puffed upward to the sky around the clock. To visitors, it seemed an environmental hazard. To the natives, it meant jobs, money, food on the table, and a traditional way of life. On those days that I wore a white shirt to school, it would be dark and sooty when I got home. But the support the town gave the coaches was strong and consistent. They wanted a winning team and they were willing to do everything in their power to get one. I was the assistant football coach and on one of those searing hot September afternoons in the fall of 1951, I stood in the dusty grass and watched the grid candidates file out of the dressing room for their first practice. This was the first time I ever saw Bevo Francis. But Bevo was not really a football player. His sport was basketball. The local fans already knew that. All you had to do was stop in McGreenhan's Restaurant in downtown Wellsville, order pie and coffee, and they would gather around. One by one, fan after fan, the locals told me that Bevo was the best basketball prospect in the history of Columbiana County. This was a hot bed of basketball fervor. Locals still talked about a game in 1906 when nearby East Liverpool won a national championship in basketball.

When I looked at the situation—a 6'9" star player, intense community support—I knew I had come upon the chance of a lifetime, the opportunity to front a team that would achieve notoriety. In the year I coached at Wellsville, the team won twenty-three times and lost twice. Bevo averaged 31 points per game. In that one year he made every all-Ohio team. No other player in Ohio high school history ever made that achievement. Because of his age he never played in his senior year.

In May of 1952, a few months before Richard Nixon's famous Checkers speech, my wife and I left Wellsville for Laramie, Wyoming. That summer I completed the require-

His outstanding games in high school are listed below:

		Wellsville	Bevo	
Mingo Junction	41	84	44	*
East Palestine	41	74	41	o
Carrollton	21	69	42	*
Lisbon	21	37	25	*
Carrollton	31	88	45	*
Alliance	50	79	57	*
Canton Central	42	86	50	*
Barnsville	58	96	54	

*   outscored entire opposing team
o   ties entire opposing team

1951-52 Wellsville High School team with 23-2 season record
Bevo Francis, number 32, is pictured with his coach, Newt Oliver who is
seated in front of him.

13

ments for a Master of Science Degree in Public Health and Physical Education. There at the University of Wyoming, I studied basketball under Ev Shelton. He was an outstanding coach who, in 1943, had won the NCAA championship with a team led by a brilliant point guard named Kenny Sailors. My master's thesis was about the history of basketball and the art of free-throw shooting. The free-throw shot is a vital component in basketball that usually determines which team will win in close contests. Earlier that year I had talked with Don Allen, the only Rio Grande alumnus who had enough money to support a basketball program. We met at his headquarters in Buffalo, New York. I asked him if he would finance the program at his alma mater if I were offered the coach's position there. Allen was the world's largest Chevrolet dealer with a string of agencies that ran down the East coast as far as Miami. He had been born on the Rio Grande campus, was a trustee of the college, and had, more than once, given the college enough money to keep its doors open. Allen, a man who had started as a used car salesman in Gallipolis, Ohio, was a financial wizard who knew the value of promotion and public relations. He was interested in anything that would help Rio Grande stay afloat. At that time, most people thought Rio Grande was a city in Texas and no one outside the region could pronounce the name properly. Allen knew this and wanted the name to become known across the United States and the world if it were possible. My meeting with Allen was an unforgettable experience.

As I waited anxiously in the lobby of Don Allen's office, I wondered how he would take to my plans. We both knew the college had little going for it at that time except regular prayers fitting a Baptist institution. I was thinking then the same thought I later expressed to Dean W. A. Lewis and other religious fanatics in power there. They could pray all day on Sunday and through the night but the bills would still be unpaid on Monday morning. That God helps those who helps themselves. When I sat down with Allen, I told him I thought the college was going to fail and that what I planned to do in basketball might save the college from extinction. I made my

14

pitch. Allen smiled. Then I told him if I had adequate basketball scholarship money, Rio Grande would play in the biggest arenas in the United States: Madison Square Garden, Boston Garden, Philadelphia, Pittsburgh, Miami, and others. When I told him this, he smiled again. He told me I was out of my mind to think that my plan was remotely possible. But Don Allen knew one thing. The college was losing enrollment and the American Baptist Association was about ready to pull the plug on its support. I went on. I asked for $6,000 to use for scholarships. When we ended our talk, he said he would put up $3,000. This was pretty good, half of what I asked for. And it was through this contribution that Allen became responsible for the greatest small college team ever assembled. Allen knew miracles could happen. He had produced one himself in his own business career with the slogan, "We are never satisfied until you are."

In August of 1952 the trustees of Rio Grande college met in Jackson, Ohio, and debated whether to close the school or try to squeeze out one more year on meager resources. By a close vote, they chose to go on one more year. Had the vote gone the other way, my date with destiny in basketball history would have been lost forever. Before signing my contract, President Charles Davis and I had a long talk. He said that if I chose to become its basketball coach, I would possibly be the last coach Rio Grande would ever have. He said that no one will ever be able to say that we had anything to do with the demise of Rio Grande College. They could only say we presided over the burial and, since we would be the last ones out, we would turn out the lights. In January, 1952 the American Baptist Association dropped its financial support from Rio Grande.

The Baptist Association may have been gone, but the college did not let up on its rules and regulations for student behavior. Girls were required to check into their dormitory rooms by 8:00 p.m. No shorts could be worn on campus. Drink a beer and you were out. And in the summer, dormitory residents sweltered with no air conditioning. The campus

The most famous little gym in America - Community Hall, erected in 1918 on the campus of Rio Grande College - and home court of the colorful Rio Grande College Redmen.

buildings were in fair condition. The gymnasium in Community Hall, known as the Hog Pen, was clean but small. There were no showers nor running water. The heat was turned off at 6:00 p.m. no matter how cold it was.

I never expected a great deal of support as coach from the administration. Although President Davis had brought me there, he was the type of person who straddled issues and tried to see which way the wind was blowing. The type of leader who would think that if some people were for a certain issue and some people were against it, he would be for the people. Whatever that meant. I did expect cooperation and loyalty from the administration. They were pretty much with me the first season, but as time went on I felt some of them were envious of the team even though we were largely responsible for the college being able to stay open and pay its bills. In retrospect, I believe the college would have shut down during the 1952-53 academic year except for Bevo Francis and his teammates. The renown and money they brought were vital elements. In a book called *Basketball and Startling Stories Behind the Records*, Jim Benaugh titled the essay on Rio Grande, *Bevo, The Player Who Saved a College*.

When I got behind my desk in August 1952, I had six weeks to recruit a basketball team. I hit the road day and night for the next six weeks paying my own expenses. I knew the school was broke. I didn't even ask about meals, mileage, and lodging. Until Bevo scored his record breaking 116 points against Ashland, Kentucky Junior College, I used my own money to pay some of the team expenses. And my salary for the year was $3,500. Rio Grande was the alma mater of me and my wife. We wanted to see the school stay open. We were happy to share part of our income to help that happen. On my first recruiting trip, I went to Wellsville to talk to Bevo Francis. I offered Bevo a modest apartment for him, his wife, and young son, $75.00 a month for groceries, and a fifty-cent-per-hour job on campus. Reporters would ask me later if Bevo was being paid by the game or the season. To his credit, Bevo never received anything beyond what was promised. Later, when the national spotlight focused on us, we picked up a few dollars with personal appearances and speaking engagements. Another problem was that Bevo was a credit-and-a-half short of his high school diploma. John Wickline, principal of Rio Grande High School, enrolled him part time to take care of this problem. President Davis asked the Ohio College Association for permission to use Bevo in intercollegiate basketball. The OCA, having no idea it was approving the greatest scorer in the history of basketball, gave its stamp of approval. When Bevo became nationally known, the same organization questioned his eligibility. Davis responded with a copy of its letter permitting him to play college ball before completing high school. Another Wellsville student, and a teammate of Bevo, John Viscoglossi, signed on with a full athletic scholarship. Dick Barr of Ashland, Ohio, came on with a full ride: room, board, books, and tuition. Barr turned down scholarships from Ashland and Kent State. Cincinnati Chase College dropped basketball that year leaving its entire roster up for grabs. Coaches down in southwestern Ohio told me Bill Ripperger was the best of that group. He had made the All-Cincinnati team during his senior year at Norwood High School. Bill signed on even though he found it hard to adjust from the urban life in Cincinnati to village life in Rio Grande. He became the best rebounder for his height I ever saw play. Bill died in 1978, the first member of the team to go. Jack Gosett, another of my recruits from Ashland, Kentucky, told me about an all-state player from Boyd County. Jim McKenzie was an unhappy player at Marshall College where freshmen were not eligible for varsity competition. McKenzie had also been recruited by Morehead State and the legendary Adolph Rupp of the University of Kentucky. Cam Henderson, Marshall College's greatest coach, who many consider the originator of the zone defense, wanted McKenzie to team up with Walt Walowac, one of Marshall's greatest players of all time. Two starters were already at Rio Grande. Roy Moses, who had played for me at Upper Sandusky, and Wayne Wiseman. Both had played the previous year in complete oblivion. Wayne Wiseman was from Waterloo, Ohio, a village on State Route

141, about halfway between Ironton and Gallipolis. His older cousin, Stewart, had been a member of the famous Waterloo Wonders team that won state tournaments back-to-back in 1934 and 1935. The Wonders were among the most exciting teams in the history of high school basketball. The coach, Magellan Hariston, gathered up five country boys and began a style of ball that was far ahead of its time. They became famous for behind-the-back passes, jump shooting and whimsical moves. Far out on the road on cold winter nights as far away as Cleveland, when players needed a rest, he would play four, or even three, men while the other men took breaks to rest. As the fury of the game went forth, the resting players signed autographs, ate hot dogs, and played marbles. Seeing that crowds loved this, they made this kind of play their trademark. Over a two-year period they won ninety-seven games and lost three. Four of them went on to barnstorm and play professional ball in large arenas throughout the Midwest. Gallia County and the region had known fabulous basketball and I knew they were hungry for it again.

Basketball playing ran deep in the Wiseman family. Wayne was a junior at Rio Grande who had already played under two coaches. In our second practice that September, I called Wiseman on a bad pass. He shot off his mouth at me. I asked him his name and he blurted it out in an antagonistic manner, "Wiseman." I cursed and told him he was off the team for one week and that the next time he challenged my authority, he would be dropped from the team. He soon came around my way. Wiseman had learned his journeyman ball-handling long before I came to Rio Grande. With Bevo and a disciplined team, he soon became an outstanding player in his own right.

The line-up looked good. Francis, Barr, Ripperger, Viscoglossi, and McKenzie. Held over were Roy Moses and Delbert Davis. They were backed up by Bill Frasher from Lucasville, Ohio, Jack Gossett from Ashland, Kentucky, and Zeke Zempter from a wide spot in the road in Scioto County, Minford, Ohio. After this torrid recruiting period, I checked out the athletic equipment. In a musty closet in Community Hall, I found one old basketball and a set of faded uniforms. I punted. I dug deeper in the closet and found the old football equipment, aged helmets, shoulder pads, balls, and shoes left over from the 1951 football season, Rio Grande's last. I boxed the stuff up, put it in the trunk of my car, drove to a sporting goods store in Athens, Ohio, and traded it for basketball supplies. Bevo had two basketballs. We used one for practice, kept the other for games. I bought two new balls with my own money. Shoes, socks, and towels were supplied by the players. We used the old uniforms, rags that they were.

Opening practice as a coach for me was the time to set the style for the year. I gathered everyone together who had come out for the team. I told them we were going to play in the big time. We were going to hit the university circuit, play the big arenas across the United States. Neither hell nor high water would stop us. High water was truly a hazard on some of the dilapidated roads around Rio Grande. We would, moreover, see our share of hell. The promised land was only five months away. I told them not to expect anything easy, no puds would be forthcoming. No smoking, no drinking, no broken rules would be accepted.

The returning players were used to being losers. The previous year, a typical one for Rio Grande, they had won four and lost fourteen. The cheerleaders could have done better. Going back to 1946, the college had changed basketball coaches each season. Six different coaches in six years. I set about reducing the roster by my usual method. I would cut no players, but I would run them off one by one by putting them through practices they never knew existed this side of hell. Under conditions that would have caused despair in most coaches, I again asserted to the team my grandiose plan. By next March we will be the toast of the college basketball world. We will have national and international acclaim. We will play in the biggest arenas, including New York's Madison Square Garden. Wayne Wiseman, who had played for Rio Grande since 1950, asked if he could speak. I told him to go ahead. He said, "The only garden we will ever see is one with a hoe."

Some hoe. I even questioned my own sanity at times. Here I was a first-year college coach in a school with ninety-two students, thirty-eight of whom were boys. Madison Square Garden?

I could understand why the players looked bewildered, thinking this new coach is not playing with a full deck. But somehow they mustered faith in the dream that we were going to try. The feat seemed impossible. But they were willing to try. I continued to lay down the goals. We will be undefeated this season. We will average at least 100 points per game. Bevo will get half or more of the points. Bevo Francis will average 50 points per game and break every record for collegiate basketball in one season. I knew from experience that basketball fans would not pay to see five players score twenty points each but if one player got half that number they would break the doors down. In reality, the plan was simple. Far reaching, but simple.

By the time of our second practice, word had gone from player to player, to the team manager, and throughout Rio Grande that I called the shots, others conformed. My next move was to ask the college to join the National Collegiate Athletic Association service bureau at a cost of $25.00. I felt this would give us a chance for national exposure once we started our streak. Our scores would be released to news outlets across the country. The National Collegiate Athletic Association would record our statistics. At the end of our second practice in that little gym on a hot September afternoon in 1952, I sprang the trapdoor on the start of our journey into an unprecedented leap to national prominence. In front of Bevo, the managers, and the team I told them of his star potential that would be the key to world-wide acclaim. I told everyone to look around at what we have and the possibilities of what we can have for playing facilities. The players looked at a building built in 1918. It had a concrete floor and a roof that leaked like a sieve. The responsibility for keeping the place clean was ours. There was no money to hire a janitor. At one end of the gym, a stage jutted out toward the playing area. At the other end, the front entrance allowed spectators to file in under the basket and take seats in folding chairs along the three levels set aside for spectators. Our postage stamp sized dressing room contained two benches and a few folding chairs.

Practice sessions lasted two to three hours. I stressed fundamentals. I insisted on proper physical conditioning. Winning was often a matter of which team made the fewest mistakes. I worked on our schedule around the clock. The former coach left a schedule of eighteen games under contract. I began by contacting other colleges in Ohio and surrounding states. I asked for a home-and-home series, but would settle for a game on their court. I offered to play Wooster College on their court with a guarantee of $35.00. Wooster coach, Mose Hole, said later his denial was the most expensive mistake he ever made. I offered Fenn College in Cleveland a home game for $40.00. No luck. At the end of our first season, playing in Cleveland, we drew 12,000 fans. It was almost impossible to schedule four-year schools. Reluctantly, I scheduled anyone who would play. Service teams, business colleges, and junior colleges signed on. Before our first game, I had forty-two slots under contract. Wright-Patterson Air Force Base later withdrew. Frostburg State of Maryland withdrew from both games arguing that we were too strong. That left us with thirty-nine games.

For many years, Rio Grande had been a pushover for teams that would play them. Humiliation was a way of life. In one week during the 1949-50 season, they played Capitol University on Monday and lost 110-46, Marietta College on Tuesday losing 114-66, Ohio Wesleyan on Wednesday going down 115-38, and on Saturday, Morris Harvey in Charleston, West Virginia, killed them 109-59. I was determined to dish out a little humiliation myself in the coming season. I was ready to kick ass. I never substituted to hold down the score. We would never rest until we had 100 or more points on the scoreboard for Rio Grande.

I was not running a popularity contest at Rio Grande. My goal was to win and win big. To pour it on and let Bevo rack up the points. Our first game of the season was against an alumni team. Here were some worn out players who had never played in a college game with a winning coach, huffing and puffing their way to a loss of 48-116. A handful of spectators watched the game. The gate receipts were $19.50. We paid the referees $30.00. Bevo scored 44, but I was not pleased with his or the team's performance. I regret that this game was ever played. A few days later, Cumberland College of Williamsburg, Kentucky, came to the Hog Pen. At half-time we led by one point. In the dressing room, I set into the team with a verbal barrage like they had never heard before. My wife told me later that I had some of the younger players scared. I told her they were all lucky we finally won 84-75. If we had lost, taking my plan awry this early in the season, the next practice would have been nothing short of hell. Dean W. A. Lewis would have thought the devil incarnate had arrived on campus. Bevo scored 45 points. Four players on the Cumberland team fouled out trying to stop him.

When our next home game came around, Sue Bennet College of London, Kentucky, came to the village. As always needing money, we raised the price of admission from fifty to seventy-five cents. The few fans we had threw a fit. I told some of the loud-mouth objectors they would be watching history in the making and soon they would be begging for tickets. One man said when that day came you wouldn't be able to get tickets at any price. That day was not too far in the future. We started slow against Sue Bennet. At the half, we slithered into the locker room with a ten-point lead. In the cramped dressing room, I kept quiet for two or three minutes. Then all hell broke loose. I kicked a stack of coat hangers lying on the floor. Hangers flew in every direction. You could have heard a pin drop. I told them what I thought of their performance. They looked like the teams Rio Grande had seen in the past. They were a sorry-ass bunch, in every respect. I gave them an ultimatum. Perform up to your capabilities and beat this team by at least twenty points or we will practice all night. The players knew I wasn't joking. We won the game 121-99. By a slim margin of two-points, the team spared seven hours of practice. Bevo scored 58 points, but he hit only sixty-nine percent of his shots. He was, at least, showing improvement. Rumors were also circulating that some players were going to quit the team. I gave the team this message: If you want to quit, pack up and get out. I have other players lined up to take your scholarships. Everyone stayed on. Afterwards, I felt a little guilty for pushing them close to exhaustion.

Two days later, we returned to action against Waynesburg College of Pennsylvania. When they arrived on campus and parked their cars in the Community Hall parking lot, they were talking trash against the Rio Grande Redmen. I happened to be walking across the street in front of Frank Allen's store as the Waynesburg players were going from their cars to Community Hall. I was only twenty-eight years old and did not look mature enough to be a college coach. I had Levis on and, maybe, fifteen cents in my pocket. I heard one of their players ask their coach, "Why didn't you schedule someone who could at least give us some competition? These farmers won't even give us a good workout, let alone be competitive." The coach and the other players laughed. I laughed, too. I knew that with an attitude like that, we could slaughter them. The Waynesburg players gathered in our small cafeteria and continued their smart-ass comments. "This is Podunk University," "I wonder if the cows will be out of the barn we'll be playing in?" "I sure hope they don't ask us to shovel manure before the practice game gets under way," were typical comments. I was incensed, and by the time our team met in the dressing room I was boiling. Bevo and the other players had heard some of the disparaging remarks. One of my players suggested that we put some color in the game. He asked if we could go out on the floor dressed as farmers in bibbed overalls. Always coaching to entertain, as well as win, I gave my approval to warm up in overalls carrying hay forks and manure shovels. The crowd of one-hundred-ten went wild. When the referees blew the whistle to start the game, we discarded our costumes and began a fast ball-pass routine in our faded, worn-out uniforms. This game was the turning point in our quest for perfection. We hit forty out of forty-six free throws.

I had not forgotten that in the fall of 1947 Waynesburg had beaten Rio Grande 56-0 in football. My goal was to win this game by a greater point spread than our football team had been beaten. But we had to settle for a thirty-eight-point difference. We beat them 108-70. Later, the Waynesburg coach told officials of the Dunkel Rating system that this was a practice game. I sent a copy of our contract to them to verify the game's legitimate status. This was the game that enabled Rio Grande to make the transition from a good small college team to Division One caliber.

For weeks I had been calling Dave Diles of the Associated Press in Columbus urging him to attend one of our games. I told Diles that he would be the first regional reporter to get a look at a team that was on the make. I had known Diles for several years. He was from nearby Middleport, Ohio. and, as a sports reporter for the *Gallipolis Daily Tribune*, he had covered Rio Grande when I was a player there. So the night we played Waynesburg, Diles was in the audience. He carried a concealed stop watch to see whether we had a rigged clock to extend the game beyond forty minutes played in four quarters. Diles told me later that he thought it was impossible to score the way we were scoring in legitimate periods. He was not the type of reporter who would tolerate a sham. Diles told me he was impressed. He assured me that henceforth we would receive our fair amount of lines over the AP wires. I asked him to be sure the news went out nationwide. Diles smiled. He later stated that Newt Oliver was the most aggressive and determined coach he ever saw.

In the early 1950s Dayton University was a national contender every season under head coach, Tom Blackburn. With four victories under our belts, we next faced their freshman team. Don Donoher, who later became head coach there, said that the freshman team was the greatest group of raw talent the University had ever recruited. This team was spiked by seven-foot center, Bill Uhl, who would later make the All-American first team. Dayton double-teamed Bevo throughout the contest, but we were not a one-man team that night. All

When Bevo Francis elevated his 6'9" body for his deadly jump shot, defenders were at his mercy. He is shown scoring two of his 69 points against Wilberforce. Roy Moses, number 27 was waiting on the rebound that never came.

five Rio Grande starters scored in double figures. Bevo out-scored Uhl 35-10. Next came an old rival. The Redmen always played Wilberforce University. They were good to us, scoring 71 to our 111. Bevo's 69 was just two points short of their total effort. Bevo, however, had not reached Rio's all-time single scoring record, eighty-seven, set by Jack Duncan in 1941.

The day after the Wilberforce game, we piled into our two old station wagons, one a gift from Don Allen, the other on loan from a Gallipolis radio station. We drove east all day on winding U. S. Route 60 through the West Virginia hills to Bluefield. Early in the game, Bevo picked up four personal fouls by what looked like some home cooking from the refe-rees. I benched him, saved him for later. Bevo did pick up a record though. With 21 points in twenty-two minutes on the floor, he made his lowest collegiate score. Roy Moses got twenty-three and, for the first and last time, Bevo was out-scored by another team member. Still, I was determined to play Bevo every minute of each game. Unlike many coaches, I would never bench the first team when we had a comfortable lead. There was no way you could ever set national records if you let up on your aggressive play. But I should point out, Bevo never fouled out one time.

We drove back to Rio Grande on fumes. With no money for motel rooms, we had to rock and roll through the night on ancient roads that followed old wagon trails. One-hundred-seventy-five miles, one way. Bevo spent the Thanksgiving holidays playing nine ball pool at the B and B pool room in Gallipolis and with his family. The other boys, all single, went home for a traditional dinner. When we got back together and got the pounds worked off, we traveled to Granville, Ohio, to play Denison University. This game was normally Denison's first game of the season with no return home game at Rio Grande. They were accustomed to using us as a tune-up game, not much more than a scrimmage. For them to whip the Redmen was a given. As soon as the athletic shoes started to squeak on the polished hardwood, they put three men on Bevo: 6'7" Don DeJong, 6'5" Bob Jones, and 6'6" Jim Cope. They held Bevo to 26 points. But by passing off to McKenzie and Moses, we won 88-78.

Our next game, the ninth of the season, was played at Marietta, Ohio. Again, we loaded up our station wagons and headed north up State Route 7 following the Ohio River. We had finally begun to get used to one another on the road and in cramped quarters. Wayne Wiseman—always sexy with a wide smile and a closet full of rayon shirts in pastel colors—demanded we tune in Johnny Ray's song _Cry_ on the radio while the rest of the boys were outvoting him to get redneck music like the Delmore Brothers singing _Blues Stay Away From Me_. In the Marietta game, we led at the half 45-34. Not too good. During the second half, Wiseman and McKenzie, who controlled our offense from their positions as guards, were fouled out by the referees. We won by three points. Out of two seasons, this was the most one-sided officiating we encountered. I told the Pioneers' athletic director and coach after the game that the Redmen would never play there again. I had been a student at Marietta during the summer of 1949 and admired the college. No more. The next night we took our record of 9-0 to Beckley College in West Virginia. We beat them 90-71. Bevo got 46.

We were averaging ninety-eight points per game. Bevo was shooting 43 percent, seven below my goal. The national press continued to ignore us. Our next game was with California State College, which was located in Pennsylvania. Bevo came within one point of beating the entire team. Bevo picked up 72 points as we won 105-73. Other than Dave Diles, the only other reporter giving us any attention was Homer Alley of the _Gallipolis Daily Tribune_. Going on a road trip through eastern Kentucky, we again played Sue Bennet College in London, Kentucky. They had played us tough in Community Hall, but this time they went down 114-68. As we came back through Morehead, Kentucky, I thought it was a shame we were not playing them. When I tried to book them earlier, the athletic director didn't even answer my letter. The following summer, he came to Rio Grande in person requesting home-and-home games. I turned him down. We were limited to twenty-five games, anyway. But I didn't forget his previous snub. A few days later, back at Community Hall, we played a weird game against Steubenville College. Every few minutes the lights went out. The janitor, Earl Davis, had to stand next to the fuse box and insert new ones a dozen times. Still, we hit 100 points for the seventh time. Bevo got 50 points as we went on to win 107-58. Even playing at this level we did not always fill Community Hall. I began to wonder what would happen if Bevo scored 100 points of his own. The players were still eating hamburgers and kept asking me where those steaks I promised them were.

After the Steubenville game we went back to Kentucky for a three-game spread. When we played Pikeville College there, I noticed that the boys had trouble holding on to the ball. Although I knew better, I began to wonder if they had split a six-pack of longnecks when I was not looking. Turned out that the game ball had been inflated to twice its normal pressure. Pikeville had practiced all week with a ball like that. But talent overcame chicanery. We won 72-52. At Lees College in Jackson, we skunked them 102-64. Bevo was a one-man scoring machine that night. With 76 points, he outscored the entire Lees team. The final score was 102-64. During this game, a fat man sat at the end of our bench roaring with leather lungs, "Give the ball to Bevo." After each yell he spat tobacco juice on the floor. I heard later that he had bet $50.00 that Bevo would score 50 points. Fifty for fifty was his cry. I'm glad he won his bet. As mean as he looked, if Bevo had been cold he might have whipped the whole team. We wound up this series at Cumberland College in Williamsburg. We beat them by twenty-nine points. On the way home, while passing through Salt Lick, Kentucky, one of our cars was struck broadside by another car. No player was hurt seriously, but I can still see Bill Ripperger with his glasses broken and blood running down his face.

After the Christmas break of 1952, Jim McKenzie never returned to campus. I drove down to Ashland, Kentucky, to find out what was wrong. I found him there in his mother's living room picking out riffs on an old Gibson guitar. He was tense. He told me he was tired of playing the role of decoy, feeding the ball to Bevo. Inside, I knew where he was coming from. Had I been a player instead of the coach, I might have felt the same way. I made an honest effort once again to explain my system to him and that when we began to play Division One teams he would get his share of the shots. Our shot at getting national recognition depended on Bevo getting his 50 points. McKenzie, one of the last great two-hand set shooters, came back in a few weeks and later hit four out of five against Villanova in the Philadelphia arena from the center of the playing court.

At this point in our schedule, we had scored 1,558 points in sixteen games to our opponents' 1,101. Bevo had accumulated 743 points for a 46.5 per cent average. We had not lost a game. I continued to call Dave Diles asking him to press forward with his stories. On December 20, 1952, my persistence finally paid off. He sent out a story called "The Siege Gun of the Rio Grande" over the A.P. wires. This is that story:

> A five-foot, nine-inch man and a six-foot, nine-inch "boy" arrived in this little southern Ohio community the same day last September.

> Together, in three short months, they've made the entire nation sit up and take notice of the three-ring basketball show at Rio Grande College.

> The little fellow who gets the show on the road is Newt Oliver, a sawed-off, hot-tempered coach in his first year in the college ranks. He's aged 29.

> The center-ring attraction—and what an attraction he is—is Clarence (Bevo) Francis, a towering freshman who flicks in points at the unbelievable rate of better than 47 per game.

With Rio Grande's schedule only one-third completed at 15 straight wins, Believe-It-or-Not Bevo has scored 709 points. And he's not even out of high school!

Bevo came to Rio Grande needing a couple of high school credits. So along with his college work, he's taking courses at Rio Grande High School and will graduate in January.

Bevo's success story is one of the strangest.

The shy, 20-year-old kid was an anemic, scrawny lad who had to stay out of school two years.

Early in his teens, his health improved. Then, in an old barn near Bevo's home in Hammondsville in Jefferson County, the talent that has made him the nation's leading collegiate scorer began to show itself. Bevo tells it this way:

"Eight or nine of us boys would work after school, doing most everything, to make some money. Pete Cope let us make a basketball court in his hayloft [sic] and we'd help him out on the light bill.

"We'd go up to the barn every Friday night and wouldn't come out again until Sunday night—playing basketball most of the time. We'd even buy food and take it up there, and we slept in the hay."

The barn-basketball went on for three years. Bevo said some of the games with teams from surrounding communities drew "more people than the high school games."

Bevo admits the "week-end encampments" in the old barn may sound a little far-fetched, but townspeople—who should know—swear it's true.

Bevo played but one year of high school basketball due to a transfer and eligibility mix-ups. That one was at Wellsville, under Oliver. But in that one year, he scored 776 points in 25 games against some of the toughest competition the state afforded. He made the All-Ohio team and became the first schoolboy athlete in the state's history to win a Helms Athletic Foundation award for basketball achievement.

A 195-pounder who wears size 13 shoes, Bevo had lucrative offers from 60-odd colleges and universities. Why, then, did he enroll at Rio Grande, a college with only 94 full-time students?

"One year under Newt at Wellsville made me want more. So, when he came here, so did I," Bevo explains.

Oliver said he told bashful Bevo "You'll be better off at a big school, and you're sure to make All-American." But even that didn't convince Bevo. He says he doesn't regret his decision.

Oliver wasn't just another player himself in his college days. While attending Rio Grande, Newt set a national record of 291 free throws in one season (It was broken last year by Seattle's Johnny O'Brien) and holds the Ohio record for the most points scored in one season with 725.

Those 725 points, scored in 1947-48, made Newt the country's top scorer that season and won him a Helms award.

Newt is sure big Bevo will break all existing individual scoring records, including Paul Arizin's 85 points in one game with Villanova in 1949 and Jack Duncan's 87 set with the same Rio Grande college in 1941. Arizin holds the

NCAA major-college scoring record and Duncan the NCAA small-college mark.

Francis figures Newt's scoring prowess helps his coaching. "It's a big difference playing under a coach you know was a great player himself. He doesn't just tell you how to do things—he shows you."

Through the first 13 games this season, Rio Grande had averaged more than 100 points per game.

Despite the close relationship between the two, Bevo is just another player when it comes to playing basketball. Newt claims he once made the big boy run 300 laps around the basketball court for failure to follow orders.

Bevo and 18-year-old Mary Chrislip were married while in high school. They have a four-month-old son, Frank Jeffrey, and—wouldn't you know it?—Bevo bought the little tyke a basketball for Christmas.

Bevo, who neither smokes nor drinks, spends much of his spare time in Oliver's apartment, replaying past games.

Francis, who hits 60 percent of his field goal attempts and 90 percent of his free throws, had his best night Friday night against Lees College at Jackson, N.Y. He whipped in 76 points. Against California (Pa.) Teachers he whipped in 72 points on 27 fielders and 18 free throws (he missed four charity tosses).

After Francis scored 46 in Rio's 108-70 win over Waynesburg, Waynesburg coach Jim Haddick said, "Bevo can do everything Mark Workman (All-America last year at West Virginia) could do and better." West Virginia defeated Waynesburg the following week by 16 points.

In the classroom he is a co-operative student who doesn't cut classes and turns in every assignment. He carries a 2.5 average in his college work.

Charles E. Davis, Rio Grande president, said "Francis is not a prima donna. Instead, he's a big asset both to the team and to the school. I'm awfully glad he's on our side."

The acceptance of the story by thousands of A.P. subscribers across the United States and around the world was tremendous. Other news services such as United Press and the International News Service also picked up the news. We had arrived at the land of opportunity. We had left the wilderness of a nondescript college in the middle of nowhere on the border of the Bible Belt.

When we came back on a bleak January day in 1953, we practiced in the Hog Pen long and hard getting ready to take on Findlay College. Playing without McKenzie, we were not as potent. Findlay's defense collapsed on Bevo at every opportunity. Still, we won 91-88, and Bevo scored 44. Findlay College had a 6' 10" player named Herk Wolfe who had been a first team college All-American. The Redmen were impressed but not intimidated. Wolfe scored 27 points while holding Bevo to 44 in front of a crowd that spilled out onto the playing floor. A sports writer wrote that Bevo could shoot but he played little defense. My response was that all Babe Ruth could do was hit home runs. A reporter for the Findlay paper wrote:

Amazingly, unbelievably accurate, the tall graceful Bevo located the basket 14 times in 25 shots from the field and converted 16 gift shots to run his total year's point production to 787 in 17 games. Francis was not without gifted playmates. Wayne Wiseman and Roy Moses in particular worked with the smoothness of talented pros.

As January rolled by, I wondered whether I could fulfill my promise to the team that we would hit the big time before the season was over. We would just have to see. I looked at my calendar and saw that our next game was with Ashland Junior College of Kentucky. An historical game lay just ahead. The Redmen defeated Ashland 150-85. Bevo got 116 points. This was the biggest break a small college team ever received in the history of the game. We scored 4 points per minute. Even more astonishing was the fact that Bevo had scored only 61 points through the third quarter. Shooting from every angle, he scored 55 points in ten minutes. Playing under today's rules which allows a player a bonus shot if he makes his first free-throw attempt and the three-point field goal, Bevo would have scored at least 135 points. Once the story reached the newspapers and television shows around the world, it became sheer bedlam. I went without sleep for the next twenty-four hours taking telephone calls from across the United States and foreign countries. A dream had come true. No longer would my wife Maxine and Bevo's wife Jean be forced to wash the team's uniforms in the one bath we shared. No longer would I have to spend my own money to support the team. No more hotdogs and hamburgers on Sundays. We were ready for filet mignons.

Overnight, the sleepy village of Rio Grande was turned into a media frenzy. The nation needed a hero and Bevo Francis was a prime candidate. The quiet Francis, a humble farm boy from a poor family, was perfect for the role. Hereafter, everywhere we played, fans would be lined up for tickets and autographs and the news media would be ever on the increase. Three days after the astonishing game at Rio Grande, *Life* magazine reporters and photographers arrived on campus to do a pictorial review of Bevo and the team. They would have been there sooner but they could not find the place. National reporters had to fly into either Columbus, Ohio, or the cities of Huntington or Charleston, West Virginia. And the West Virginia cities had small airfields that had been scraped off mountaintops. The only sour note to develop from this great event was that President Davis told me to inform the *Life* reporters that he was available for an interview and pictures. I told the *Life* reporters and they said they were interested only in Bevo and the team. When I told Davis this, he became incensed. Although I did not understand it at the time, a schism was beginning to develop between the team and me and certain campus individuals. We had in reality become too big for our surroundings.

Now with nineteen games under our belt and undefeated, our scoring was piling up. The Redmen had 1,918 points. Our opponents had scored 1,365. Bevo had 966 and his average per game was 50.8 per outing. When we played our twentieth game in Gallipolis against the Wright Patterson Air Force base team, it was hard for fans to get tickets. The gymnasium seated 750. A thousand people were crowded in. Hundreds were turned away. During the pre-game activities, Bevo was named an honorary city manager and presented a key to the city. The Kittyhawks from Lockbourne, Ohio, were comprised of former Division One college basketball stars such as Pete Boyles and Joe Genaro. They had formerly played for the University of Dayton team that was runner up in the 1951-52 National Invitational Tournament. Also playing for them were Tony Durwowicz, a former Georgetown player, Ben Roescher, a Rutgers star, and Bob Armstrong, and All-Ohio college star. We were impressed. But we knew that if they placed two or three defenders on Bevo and left the other players open we could score. Bevo got 55 points under heavy guard but the rest of the Redmen team pitched in for a final score of 113-85. This game proved that Division One players were unable to shake our quest.

The next night we played Bliss Business College at Columbus. They brought in players from all over central Ohio. Dave Dillahunt was recruited off the Ohio State campus. I had bragged earlier that before the year was over fans would be tearing down doors to see us play. In the Bliss College game, the back door to the gym was torn off. Thousands were turned away and I had to ask the officials to keep those who had gotten in off the playing floor. People outside climbed trees to try to look into the windows for a look at Bevo. A crew from Dave Garroway's _Today_ television show out of New York City

Columbus, Ohio - 1953. With fans spilling out on the playing court, Bevo Francis sets the all time NCAA and NAIA single season scoring record with 1,072 points. In this particular game against Bliss College he scored 51 points.

was on hand to film footage for their program. We beat Bliss 101-53 and Bevo scored 51 points setting a national scoring record for one season of 1,072. Johnny O'Brian of Seattle University held the previous record with 1,051. And we had eighteen games left to play. In the last few minutes of play the Redmen put on a Globetrotter style show and the crowd went wild.

The Redmen's next stop was at the Groveport High School gymnasium against Lockbourne Air Force base. The airmen were coached by a man who later became famous, or infamous, with the New York Yankees baseball team, George Steinbrenner III. Lockbourne had a 17-2 winning record including a string of nine straight. Reporters showed up from across the country. Milton Gross of the New York Post was there to begin a series of stories on Bevo and the team. As Lockbourne came out to warm up, I noticed their numeral uniforms were an off-white color. Our uniforms were white, nearly the same as theirs. In less than three minutes we made two passes to Lockbourne players. I called time-out and told the officials to order the opponents to change to a contrasting color. They told Steinbrenner that the rules required home teams to wear dark uniforms. He was hot but he made the change. Bevo was cold and scored only 36 points, but we won 84-50.

Since we were beginning to get national attention, I decided to begin asking our opponents for a $1,000 guarantee or 65 per cent of the gate, whichever was greater. Our next game against Cedarville College had been arranged by Jack Myers, the manager of Troy Arena. Seven-thousand-four-hundred-fifty-one people paid to get in and many free passes had been given out. Floyd Reese, who had been dismissed by Rio Grande the year before I was hired, was Cedarville's coach. It was my feeling that he thought I was partially responsible for his short tenure at Rio Grande. From the beginning of the game, it was apparent that he had no intention of having his team play ball. When they got possession of the ball, the team stood around the center of the court passing the ball back and forth. They made no attempt to move toward their basket and score. I called a time-out and told the Redmen that if Cedarville does not want to play basketball just let them stand out there. I felt the crowd and the building management would take care of the problem. My team came to our bench, put on sweat suits, signed autographs, and held interviews. At the half, we were leading 21-7. Fans were throwing coins and paper cups on the playing floor. They had paid to see Bevo play ball. Sixty-eight press credentials had been issued to newspaper reporters. Several magazine writers and _Paramount News of the Day_ were there. A _Life_ magazine photographer was taking pictures. The arena was overflowing its 5,500 seating capacity. Outside, there was a five-mile traffic jam choking the streets around the arena with police telling drivers to turn around because they could not get in anyway. During intermission, Bryan Hollinger, Cedarville's athletic director, asked coach Reese if he realized that 7,500 fans were going to be asking for their money back. I told both of them to stop this farce or their home game with us will be cancelled. Hollinger probably knew that the crowd had spent about $10,000 and that our share would be $6,500. In 1996 dollars our share would amount to about $36,000. Reese told his boys to play, but the speed was only slightly picked up. We started the third quarter with our Globetrotter style show. The fans were delighted and when the game was over gave us a standing ovation. We beat them 66-29. With 38 points, again, Bevo outscored the opponent's entire team. After twenty-three games, Bevo had 1,146 points for an average of 49.8 per cent and we were still undefeated. The next issue of _Life_ magazine featured a story on Bevo and the team with pictures from the Cedarville game and the Rio Grande campus. This game was written about in newspapers across the country and was known as the game that produced a deep freeze. It also froze Bevo below his per game average.

The next day following the Cedarville game, I received a phone call from my friend, Si Burick, sports editor of the _Dayton Daily News_. He wanted us to play at the University of Dayton Field House. He offered us $2,500. I asked for more and we finally agreed on $4,000. The game became a benefit performance with the Cincinnati Bible Seminary for the March of Dimes polio effort. And even in an arena that would not accommodate all who wanted to attend, $25,000 was raised for the polio charity. We won 79-54.

The Redmen's next game was another March of Dimes benefit sponsored by the _Zanesville News_. In a game sold out weeks ahead at the Zanesville Auditorium with Mountain State of West Virginia, we beat them 131-83. Bevo scored 66 points hitting from far and wide with every shot in the book. He made one shot at close range between his legs. The crowd went into an uproar and gave him a standing ovation. Near Zanesville in my home town of Byesville, in a pool room over the A&P store on the main drag, pool sharks played pill pool as they listened to the game on the radio. Side bets covered the point spread we would pile up and Bevo's total. At Byesville High School, Dutch Sichna, the local high school all-star, practiced his assortment of shots. Sichna later turned down several Division One scholarships to take a professional slot with the Boston Whirlwinds. They paid him $600 a month with room and board thrown in. Bevo scored 66. This game was covered by *Paramount News-of-the Day* and Metro-Goldwyn Mayer's news film which was shown in theaters across the country. With the recognition we were receiving, Rio Grande had an opportunity to secure additional money and students. They, however, failed to capitalize on this phenomenal team.

Next we went to Huntington, West Virginia, to compete against the Beckley College Blue Eagles at the Huntington Memorial Field House. We gathered another sold-out crowd there in the hotbed of West Virginia basketball, home of Marshall College's Thundering Herd coached by Cam Henderson, master of the fast break. We won 102-69 with Bevo collecting 46 points. His season average had increased to 52. We moved on up the Ohio River in our two old station wagons to Toronto, Ohio, a short distance from Bevo's home town to play Steubenville College. The auditorium with 2,200 seats had been sold out for weeks. A few hours before game time, a local radio station announcer told local listeners that standing-room-only tickets would go on sale at 6:30 p.m. Two-thousand people showed up for the few spaces available. We won 78-65 in a lackluster performance.

Sports reporters around the country debated the team's quality and whether Bevo deserved the adulation he was getting. Si Burick of the *Dayton Daily News* wrote:

> . . . One newspaper author has taken it upon himself to disagree with the view here that Francis, whom I have never seen, must be a genuine wonder. His reasoning (?) is that Bevo has rolled up his points against inferior opposition. That's the same as saying you shouldn't count U. D.'s victories over Manchester and Gustavus Adolphus in this season's results because they happened to represent inferior opposition.

Most scoring records have been established against opposition that was inferior on the given day. If the opposition was superior, then it wouldn't be so vulnerable as to give up that many points.

The most important angle where Rio Grande's Francis is concerned is this: He is doing something in the way of basketball scoring that no other player has ever done before. Rio Grande is playing the kind of schedule it normally plays. Lou Gehrig didn't hit his four home runs in one ball game off Walter Johnson or Lefty Grove. And the 60 homes that Babe Ruth hit in 1927 included some off pitchers who weren't worthy of their big league uniforms.

The next game was in Wellsville, a homecoming celebration for Bevo and me. We had left Wellsville only nine months earlier. The Booster's Club staged a three day celebration in honor of Bevo and the team. A parade down the main street started the festivities. Three-thousand people lined the parade route. On Monday, 2,000 fans were jammed into the Wellsville High School gym taking all seats and standing room. A special celebration was presided over by Dr. S. A. Daw wherein Bevo was presented his high school diploma. Bevo had finished his credit-and-a-half at Rio Grande High School and transferred them to Wellsville. On game day, Wellsville High School students were dismissed early to join in the activities. City Mayor, C. C. Leatherberry, presented Bevo a key to the city. Myron Weiss, President of the Chamber of Commerce, complimented Bevo for his national acclaim and the honor he was bringing to his home town. Before the game with Pikeville, Kentucky, their coach asked me if we would be playing them next season. I told him I would deal with that when the season was over. He pulled out a set of drawn-up contracts and told me to sign or this game was off. I told him he could damn well suit himself, put his team on the floor or go home. They played. After the game I congratulated him on the fact that his team had beaten Bevo 62-61. The Redmen and Bevo together scored 97.

We had now begun to receive some critical publicity from selected sports writers around the country. When asked about our schedule, I told reporters we played the same teams the college had traditionally played and that next year we would play any Division One team that would let us in including the Ohio State University. Many skeptical reports said that if we scheduled major ball clubs we would be blown away. After our homecoming game at Wellsville, the players felt they were making a considerable financial contribution to the college including money for faculty paychecks. Away from the campus we were idolized wherever we went. But things were different back on campus. Selected members of the administration felt we were harming the college. A few of them were reluctant to make eye contact with me and members of the team, often refusing to speak to us. Jealousy and envy, it seemed to me, were motivational factors. Even some leading citizens of the community began to treat us with the coolness of a January snowstorm. Hard as it was to fathom, at some home games in the Hog Pen a few locals cheered for our opponents. I often felt like a 12 o'clock girl in an 8 o'clock town.

Since its birth in Christian fervor seventy years earlier, Rio Grande College had been a sedate little school where nineteenth century values prevailed. They fielded sports teams, but they never played a big role in campus life. Life there was focused on studies in the humanities leading to teaching certificates and pastoral positions. Before Charles Davis, all presidents had been ministers in their own right. The philosophy of idealism was deeply rooted in Rio Grande's tradition. Leaders believed in the ancient idea that scholars should draw themselves away from the day-to-day hubbub of the realities of life. Ivory towers in the Appalachian plateau. They believed in revelation and pure reasoning as the way to find answers to the questions of how to live the good life. They looked to the Bible and the ancients for words to lead them through the crises of life. They wore suits and wingtip shoes. These campus leaders and their supporters were unprepared to deal with the reality that basketball was literally Rio Grande's only claim to fame. Conservative as they were, they began to long for the good old days when the biggest news on campus was the program at the weekly meeting of the College Christian Association. They were facing a dilemma of the sharpest kind. The team was taking Rio Grande to the national spotlight and bringing in money. Idealists were going to have to confront pragmatists—sticking with ancient principles and going down with the ship or coming of age to the twentieth century where if ideas worked they were deemed appropriate. Were the sides drawn so sharply that there were no hopes for a compromise? President Charles Davis was the man in the vortex.

After a five-day rest, the Redmen played Mayo State at Middleport, Ohio, on February 8, 1953, in a return engagement. Increased ticket prices sent many fans away. Only 425 people turned out to see Bevo score 60 points in our 126-98 victory. Next we were scheduled to play Cedarville College again at its home base. But because a large crowd was expected, the game was moved to Springfield, Ohio. Again, Cedarville did not really compete with us and Bevo with 51 points outscored its team. The final score was 104-48. We had boosted our wins to thirty-one straight and Bevo had 1,515 points averaging 49.

Our next game was a return event with Mountain State College at the Parkersburg, West Virginia, Memorial Field House. The arena seated 3,000 and there was a large area for standing-room spectators. Bevo slipped to 37 points in this game. The final score was 116-65 in our favor. I consoled Bevo after the game telling him that he, like all players, would have peaks and valleys in his performance. The press was continually asking me whether we would consent to play major teams. My answer was that next season we would play every major college we could fit into our schedule. The total enrollment at Rio Grande had slipped to eight-eight, many of whom were young women. We were possibly the smallest four-year-degree-granting institution in the country. With eight games left on our season schedule, we played Bliss College of Columbus again. This game was played at Wellston, a few miles north of Rio Grande. It seemed we were playing an entirely different team. None of the players was recognizable from the first time we played them. The game was a sell-out and we won 105-69. Bevo got 49 points. In the meantime, a group of civic leaders from Louisville, Kentucky, visited Rio Grande. They wanted us to play a forthcoming game there. I agreed to move our next game there for a guarantee of $4,000. (This was the equivalent of $24,000, 1996 dollars). However, President Davis informed me that we were to play this game in Portsmouth, Ohio. A college trustee had a friend there who belonged to the local Kiwanis Club and Davis wanted to accommodate him. There would be no guarantee. The Kiwanis Club set the ticket price at $3.00. In today's money this would be $18.00. Portsmouth was a basketball town but its working class residents could not afford to pay this kind of money for a game. A small crowd turned out to see us again play George Steinbrenner's Lock-bourne Air Force team in Grant Gym. Bevo scored 47 points to break a local record that I set in 1947 with 38. We won the game 95-80. Playing there to please the administration cost the college several thousand dollars it could have used to pay expenses. We next played a return game with Lees College at Chillicothe, Ohio. Bevo outscored the Lees team with his 63 points. We won 128-57. After this game, we prepared for an appearance in the Cincinnati Garden against Wilberforce University. More than 8,500 fans turned out to see us play. They were not disappointed. With thirty seconds left on the clock, Bevo broke the Garden's scoring record of 49 points. He racked up 52 in our 100-61 win. It was a special game for Bill Ripperger, a graduate of nearby Norwood High school. His former principal and coach presented him with a large trophy. Going against our standard procedure, I told the team to give the ball to Ripperger at every opportunity. I wanted him to shine in his home town. Bill got 19 points. We won 100-51. Bevo got 52. After our game, the first on a double-bill with the University of Cincinnati playing Kent State University, more than half of

44

BEVO TO HEADLINE TRIPLE-HEADER

45

the 8,500 in attendance left. This was a great tribute to a small college team who, in previous years, could not have drawn enough fans to fill a high school gym. After our game, Bevo and I appeared on the "Waite Hoyt Hall of Fame" television show in Cincinnati. Hoyt asked Bevo if he intended to stay at Rio Grande or transfer to a major college team. He told Hoyt that he would stay his four years at Rio Grande because, more than anything else, he liked the people there. The next day, a reporter for a Cincinnati newspaper reported that Bevo and his teammates were everything they were said to be and much more.

When we returned to the Rio Grande campus, President Charles Davis told me that he and others felt the team's publicity was hurting the college. I told him that anytime there is a great deal of national and international reporting going on about anything, it would not all be favorable. Even if we stood on a stack of Bibles, someone would downgrade our efforts. We soon played the last game we would ever play in the Hog Pen. West Virginia's Bluefield College came over. This game was a gesture of appreciation to those fans who had supported us long before we hit the big time. A reporter writing in the *Gallia Times* newspaper wrote: "The crowd paid more money to see Bevo and company than any other gathering in Community Hall ever paid to see anything or anybody before." The Hog Pen was packed to the rafters and every inch of spectator space was used up. The Redmen won 128-73 with Bevo getting 53 points from all angles. He hit one shot from ten feet never looking toward the basket. During the last three minutes we put on a show that the *Gallipolis Daily Tribune* noted as razzle-dabble ball handling that reminded many of the Waterloo Wonders in their best moments. Next we went down to Ashland, Kentucky, to play our return game with the team that had been victim to Bevo's 116 points earlier in the season. In that era, recruiting rules were lax enough for Ashland to recruit players from the tri-state region of Ohio, West Virginia, and Kentucky. A newspaper scribe wrote that coach Bill Carter picked up any player he could in an effort to be competitive. Sam Piatt, writing for the *Ashland Daily Independent* forty years

The most colorful basketball arena in the county - the Hog Pen at Rio Grande College - was the home of the famous Rio Grande College Redmen and the nation's highest scoring performer, Clarence (Bevo) Francis, shown during an impromptu workout.

later, wrote: "Charles Hobbs, a member of the Ashland team, said that Ashland loaded up on Rio Grande with John Thomas, who had rewrote [sic] the Eastern Kentucky conference record books before graduating from Russell High School in 1946. He was said to be over 7 feet tall. Thomas stated that he never did actually enroll in the school." Young men would enroll the day of the game and withdraw the next day. Big John Thomas was offered a payment on his car for playing, a payment he never received even though he played. Adolph Rupp of the University of Kentucky had earlier tried to recruit Thomas to no avail. He did not want to go to college. Bevo got the tip-off at the start of the game and held Thomas to 4 points while scoring 25. In a hard-fought game, we won 70-63. Now our season record stood at thirty-seven wins with two games left. I was sure we could end the year with the longest winning streak in the history of college basketball. So far we had overcome a variety of teams in arenas across the region. We had suffered no major injuries nor sicknesses. We had, at times, struggled against biased referees.

The next to last game of the season was played at the Washington School gymnasium in Gallipolis against Cincinnati Bible Seminary. Bevo broke a three year scoring record during this game for the state of Ohio. This record was previously held by the University of Dayton's Donald "Monk" Meineke who, in 1954, was voted NBA rookie of the year. Bevo scored 8 points in the final twenty seconds to wind up with 59. The final score was 111-86.

The Redmen's last game of the season was scheduled against Oakland City College of Indiana. We were to play them on their home court. Our contract called for us to be paid $75. In the meantime, we got an offer to play in the Cleveland Arena for a guarantee of $2,500 or 25 per cent of the gate, whichever was greater. Knowing that the college needed money, I asked the Oakland coach to reschedule the game at their convenience and would still fulfill the $75.00 contract. Since this was Oakland's last game and would create no rescheduling problems, I was shocked when told that under no circumstances would they reschedule our game. I read the contract again and found an escape clause. It said that if either party did not honor the contract, the $75.00 would be forfeited. I sent them a check for $100. They returned it demanding $500. I was not going to pay them that much. President Davis, without consulting me, sent Oakland a check for $500. I took umbrage at this act and the hard feelings between Davis and me continued. Early in the season, I had spent my own money to keep the team going. And, suddenly, Rio Grande was giving away $500.00 when the college was so hard up it was barely meeting day-to-day expenses.

Before playing our last game of the season, Bevo and I made personal appearances on Dave Garroway's Today show and Ed Sullivan's Toast of the Town television shows in New York City. Across America Rio Grande College was receiving millions of dollars worth of free publicity. But back on campus we were being treated much like an unwanted stepchild. The authorities there did not seem to know what to do with us. After a flurry of personal appearances in New York City we took off for Cleveland. We met the rest of the team there to play our last season game in the Cleveland Arena. We played a double-header there where the second game was between John Carroll and Seton Hall. Seton Hall had already been invited to the National Invitational Tournament and we were confident that an offer to play would be forthcoming to the Redmen. My friend, Honey Russel, coach of Seton Hall and former coach of the Boston Celtics, told me that we deserved a slot in the NIT. He did, however, say that he was doubtful we would get the call because of politics and the small size of our college. Milton Cross, sportswriter for the _New York Post_, said that he had never seen as much politics being applied to keeping a team out of the tournament. I was convinced after watching Seton Hall play that we could have won the title had we been invited.

Playing that night in Cleveland against Wilberforce, Bevo was at the top of his game. He came within two points of outscoring the opposing team with 54 points. The final score was 109-55. The *Cleveland Press* described Bevo's exhibition as the ". . . greatest basketball barrage since Hank Luisetti of Stanford snowed Western Reserve under with 50 points in the late 1930's in Public Hall." Luisetti is remembered in basketball history as the player who shocked the sports world by becoming the first basketball player to use the one-hand shot in a devastating manner. Before the Seton Hall and John Carroll game got underway, hundreds of fans left the arena. They had come to see Bevo Francis perform, not Walter Dukes, the Seton Hall All-American. For the season our record was 39-0. Bevo had scored a total of 1,954 points. He had averaged 50.1 per game. He thus became the only player in the history of college basketball to average 50 points in a season. In the year 1953, Bevo scored 1,954 points. If Maryland State of Frostburg had not cancelled its home-and-home contract with Rio Grande, we would surely have ended the season 41-0 and Bevo would have passed the 2,000-point mark.

After the season was over, Bevo and I hit the chicken and peas banquet trail up to five nights per week. This enabled us to supplement our meager incomes. In my home town of Byesville, a surprise celebration was held for us at the largest banquet celebration in the village's history. A large banner reading "Welcome Home Newt Oliver" was stretched high above the main street in town. In attendance was Roy Stull, sports editor of the Cambridge, Ohio, *Daily Jeffersonian*, the village's main source of sports news. He had covered our games throughout the season. Back in Bevo's home town of Wellsville, loyal fans gathered each day to discuss and praise their first national sports idol. For the past nine months, Bevo had dominated the street talk and the coffee sessions at Pete's Restaurant in downtown Wellsville.

In the middle of March, as the crocuses began to break through the barren ground of Rio Grande's campus, the annual convention of the National Association of Basketball Coaches was called to order. Drastic changes regarding guidelines for collegiate basketball records for teams and individuals were on the agenda. The NABC not only created new guidelines, it made them retroactive. The records the Redmen established conformed to existing guidelines. To tamper with these records in a retroactive manner was an insult to the team and the game of basketball. But on a positive note, the NABC's decision compelled us to excel the following season. The NABC ruled that new standards would (1) be retroactive, and (2) eliminate games from the records that included alumni, service teams, independent teams, and any other games not played against accredited degree- granting institutions.

The coach of Pittsburgh University stated that the committee had taken in too much territory when it required that institutions be accredited. Schools are constantly going in and out of accredited status. Since Rio Grande was unaccredited, it was possible that none of our records would count. Word was going around that, one way or another, Rio Grande's records were going to be expunged. Floyd Stahl, basketball coach at the Ohio State University, said at the NABC meeting: (1) I think we, as a coaching body, should go on record as indicated here that trumped up records and records made against any kind of competition is against our principles; (2) we have to be a little careful in Ohio about saying anything derogatory about Rio Grande or Bevo Francis, who may be a great ball player. I say that because he is sort of a common people's All-American; and (3) we feel that many of the games that colleges play are against competition that is much inferior to some of our high schools. Stahl did not mention that Alcorn A&M had played fifty games against any kind of team that same season. Howard Hobson of Yale put the following motion that was adopted by the NABC: that the National College Athletic Association official records, teams and individuals, include only games between four-year-degree-granting institutions and that the policy be made retroactive. Since Rio Grande was a member of the NAIA, not the NCAA, this resolution was not of great importance. The following December in Miami, Florida, I came face-to-face with Floyd Stahl. I looked him in the eye and told him he would do well to look after his own team and stop running down the smallest and poorest college in Ohio.

This so-called anti-Bevo rule was published in newspapers and magazines around the world. Many writers and radio and television announcers said it was the most flagrant injustice in the history of sports. While the NCAA was trying to limit our stature, the headlines were adding to the legendary feats of this team that have held forth over the years. When the press asked Bevo how he felt, his response was "The people saw me score the points. They can pass all the rules they like, but the fact remains that I scored the points." My statement to the press was that from now on our statistics will be kept by the NAIA. They have accepted our team and individual records as they stand.

We were invited to an All-Star North and South game at Kansas City where Bevo was to put on a half time shooting exhibition under my direction. He hit twenty-one out of thirty shots from fifteen- and twenty-foot angles. The crowd gave

Ararat Shrine Temple

and its officers

Honor

Newt Oliver

for outstanding service participation

in the

Second Ararat Shrine Temple East-West All Star Basketball Game

for the benefit of

Shriners Hospitals for Crippled Children

Held at Kansas City, Missouri, this

twenty-eighth day of March, Nineteen hundred fifty-three

General Chairman East-West All-Star Basketball Game   Potentate Ararat Temple him a standing ovation as he left the arena. At our spring basketball banquet in Gallipolis, Dave Diles was the toastmaster and Fritz Howell, AP sports writer, was the principal speaker. Howell praised Bevo and the Redmen, pointing out that the team would forever last in the history of basketball. Bevo was presented the Don Allen trophy, an object so large it took two people to carry it. Each player was given a jacket with the design of a basketball on the front. The back read, "National Basketball Scoring Champions - 1952-53." On May 1 another banquet was held in Gallipolis sponsored by the United States Rubber Company. It gave the team its "Pro-Keds Trophy," symbolic of the most improved basketball team in the country. The award was presented by Dick Dunkel, who rated teams nationwide. He said that "... no team in the history of my rating system formulated on a mathematical model had made the improvement that Rio Grande had made in one season of play." The Redmen of the previous season had a record of 4-14. We were 39-0, the longest streak in college basketball history. Frank Leahy of Notre Dame was the main speaker. He said, "Champions are ever penalized. You must accept this as a given fact and try all the harder because of it." The next morning my wife gave birth to a baby boy whom we named John Newton Oliver II. John, now an Ohio Highway Trooper, was recently featured on a national television show regarding his work in law enforcement in which a shoot-out occurred.

After the post season hurrahs, President Davis said that the college board of trustees wanted me to come to its next meeting. I looked forward to this meeting expecting a nice pay raise and congratulations. However, in the meeting seated around a large oval table a group of men in suits looked at me with cold eyes. One of them handed me a legal-size sheet of paper that contained these new rules: (1) no sports equipment would be purchased without the consent of the college treasurer; (2) no games would be scheduled for 1953-54 without prior consent of the newly formed Athletic Council; (3) no more than twenty-five games were to be scheduled; and (4) there would be no practice before November 1. Newspaper writers began

Bevo Francis admires the Don Allen Trophy which was presented to the Rio Grange College All American. Don Allen, the worlds largest Chevrolet dealer and former Rio Grande graduate, made the trophy available. Coach Newt Oliver, the man who made it all possible is shown at left.

Coach Newt Oliver speaking at an Awards Banquet, which was
sponsored by U.S. Rubber Company, in Gallopolis, Ohio in May of 1953:
The banquet was in honor of the Redmen, who were chosen as most
improved college basketball team in America.
Frank Leahy, head coach of Notre Dame, principle speaker, is at left.

reporting that the Redmen were growing too fast and that pressure would be applied to force us back to the confines of the 150 seats in Community Hall. The following letter from B. L. Stradley of the Ohio State University arrived in President Davis' office in early May:

The Ohio State University

Columbus 10

May 1, 1953

President, Charles E. Davis
Rio Grande College
Rio Grande, Ohio

Mr. dear President Davis:

I enclose herewith a report of the Intercollegiate Athletics Committee of the Ohio College Association. This report may help you and your faculty as a general guide.

It occurs to me that additional guides or objectives should include:

1. For the participant: Development of physical vigor and desirable health habits, desirable habits of sanitation and safety.

2. For the school: Athletics should occupy a position in the school comparable to other activities. Athletics should be educational. Athletics should be an aid to school administration rather than a source of trouble.

Most conferences recognize the undue emphasis placed on athletics. Spring practices, length of season, post-season games, etc. all have been scrutinized carefully in the past two years. Length of seasons have been sharply defined, number of contests regulated, spring practices either reduced or eliminated.

Basketball has been generally confined to the period between December 1 and March 15 with practice starting November 1. Certainly not more than 22 to 25 games can be scheduled within this period without undue pressure, excessive competition, loss of school days resulting from travel.

In the case of Rio Grande College it appears that there is an abnormal condition of exploitation of an individual or individuals and that unless controls are enforced, there will be an unlimited number of games, excessive absences from classes, and undue publicity and pressure reflecting on the college. It likewise appears that the coach intends "to make the most of a good thing." You, through your Athletic Committee, must not permit the good name of Rio Grande College to be subject to attack and should definitely state (1) length of season, (2) number of contests allowed, (3) number of absences from class, and (4) financial control.

It is very important that Rio Grande College support these policies if Rio Grande hopes to continue as an Associate Member of the Ohio College Association.

Sincerely yours,

/s/ B. L. Stradley
Vice President

BLS:jg [3]

President Davis in 1951 was instrumental in making Rio Grande College an associate member of the Ohio College Association. He stated then that Rio Grande had received its first accreditation in the history of the college. This statement was wrong because the Ohio College Association was an association of colleges, not an accrediting association. Rio Grande was accredited by the State Department of Education. The North Central Association of Colleges did not admit Rio

Grande until 1969. Hell was coming to the team and me from Floyd Stahl, the Ohio State University basketball coach, a major administrator of Ohio State, other selected Ohio colleges, and the local administrators. A reporter stated: "Don't think for one minute that Ohio State and other Ohio colleges will ever let you and your team push them to the back of the sports pages while your team and Bevo are front page news." Rio Grande with eighty-eight students and one sport were bullied into accepting rules and regulations that applied only to them. The rules laid down by the Ohio College Association were singular in nature and did not apply to the rest of its members. Dirty politics. And the Rio Grande administration bought it one hundred percent. The University of Dayton scheduled thirty games. Xavier scheduled 30. Both of these schools were members of the OCA and, additionally, had teams in football, baseball, and track. I cut six games from the next season's schedule. I challenged Stahl's Ohio State team to a game giving him a chance to prove that we were a flash in the pan. He rejected the offer with the lame excuse that their schedule was full. I continued to try to book major college teams elsewhere. I was able to get the team two sets of new uniforms patterned after the East-West All-Star design. Looking to the fall with an increase in my family and my wife having to give up her teaching job, I asked the president for a $1,000 raise which would bring my salary to $4,500 for the twelve-month contract. He raised my salary $120.

The summer of 1953 gave us a chance to get away for a while and try to put the season in perspective. The team members took off to their homes looking for part-time jobs and time away from the coach. I'm sure those who chose to do so had a few cold longnecks and smoked several packs of tailormades. Chasing girls was also a major part of most team members' recreation. The coming of summer brought out the dark red azaleas that bloomed on the high banks north of the Allen House. Song birds laid eggs in their nests built in the gutters on Anniversary Hall. New students, many of them WWII veterans, checked in for the summer session seeking rooms in dormitories and tourist homes. As the days became longer, many piled into cars and headed a few miles south to Cora Dam, the site of an ancient gristmill. There was water there, parking space, and a woods that offered privacy for beer drinking and opportunities for young men to make out with reluctant, but often willing, coeds. Sometimes students cruised in toward Gallipolis, perhaps stopping at Nate Morehouse's beer joint in Addison where Burger beer was a house speciality at twenty-five cents a throw. In town, at Gilkey's Queen Bee, the All-American Tavern served drinkers, and an adjacent restaurant catered to those who wanted a hamburger or a chance to hear the sounds of steel balls hammering against bumpers on pinball machines. Up the river, three roadhouses, politely called night clubs, catered to a mix of college students and rednecks. The 7-35 Club, with live hillbilly music on weekends, attracted a working class crowd who came out to drink, fight, and pick up girls for after-closing-time rendez-vous. The Flamingo Club and the Blue Willow, further up the road at Kanagua, were less rowdy but the beer and Seven-Sevens flowed freely. Ballplayers and other students danced fast and dirty on the rosen sprinkled dance floors in these places to the sounds of Les Paul and Mary Ford's Bye Bye Blues long into the morning hours. In downtown Gallipolis, students with more money, and those dressed up with dates, were likely to stop after the movies at the Lafayette Grill located in the best hotel in town. A black bartender named Henry Doss, resplendent in his starched, white uniform, served up Singapore Slings in a stylish manner. Boys without dates lounged at the Grande Cafe, the Eagles Club, or the smoke-filled B and B Billiard Academy on 2nd Street where Bevo Francis spent many idle hours playing nine-ball pool for a quarter a game. Ministerial students were content with the pristine activities of the College Christian Association. Some did remember the epitaph on Rio Grande's second president Albanus Avery Moulton's grave on the knoll at Calvary Baptist Church in Rio Grande: "The Righteous Shall Be In Everlasting Memory." But not many.

In late May I returned to Laramie, Wyoming, where I began work on a doctor's degree in physical education. After six weeks I returned to Rio Grande to consider my next move. While in Laramie, I was offered a coaching job in the western part of the United States. A provision in the offer was that I would be able to bring Bevo and his family and that they would be provided for. When I talked this over with Don Allen, he implored me to stay at Rio Grande at least another year. He sweetened the conversation with the offer of a new station wagon. Both the college and I owed a great deal to Allen and I told him I would stay on.

All-America Way... No. 6

1952-53 ANALYSIS

Most Team Points	150
Least Team Points	66
Lowest Defensive Total	29
Highest Defensive Total	99
Highest Point Spread	65
Offensive Average	101.1
Defensive Average	68.2
Point Spread	33

MOST COLLEGE WINS ONE SEASON

No.	College	Season
39	Rio Grande	1952-53
31	Maryville (Md.) STC	1929-30
31	Pasedena College	1952-53
29	S.W. Texas Teachers College	1951-52
27	Seton Hall	1952-53
26	University of North Carolina	1923-24
26	Long Island University	1935-36
26	Holy Cross	1950-51

1952-53 WINNING STREAK SHOWING BEVO'S INDIVIDUAL SCORING

GAME	RIO	OPPOSITION		PLAYED AT	BEVO'S SCORING		
					FG	F	PTS
1.	116	Alumni	48	Community Hall	19	6	44
2.	84	Cumberland	75	Community Hall	17	11	45
3.	121	Sue Bennett	99	Community Hall	20	18	58
4.	108	Waynesburg	70	Community Hall	13	20	46
5.	93	Dayton Freshmen	89	Community Hall	9	19	35
6.	111	Wilberforce	71	Community Hall	23	23	69
7.	93	Bluefield	63	Bluefield, VA.	8	5	21
8.	88	Dennison	78	Granville, OH	10	6	26
9.	76	Marietta	73	Marietta, OH	12	13	37
10.	90	Beckley	71	Beckley, WV	14	18	46
11.	105	California State	73	Community Hall	27	18	72
12.	114	Sue Bennett	68	London, KY	19	21	59
13.	107	Steubenville	58	Community Hall	18	14	50
14.	72	Pikeville	52	Pikeviile, KY	11	3	25
15.	102	Lees College	64	Jackson, KY	27	22	76
16.	78	Cumberland	49	Williamsburg, KY	8	18	34
17.	91	Findlay	88	Findlay, OH	14	16	44
18.	150	Ashland Jr. College	85	Community Hall	47	22	116
19.	119	Mayo State	91	Paintsville, KY	21	21	63
20.	113	Wright Patterson	85	Gallipolis, OH	18	19	55
21.	101	Bliss	53	Columbus, OH	19	13	51
22.	84	Lockbourne Air Force	50	Groveport, OH	12	12	36
23.	66	Cedarville	29	Troy, OH	14	10	38
24.	79	Cincinnati Seminary	54	Dayton, OH	20	2	42

1952-53 WINNING STREAK — Continued

GAME	RIO	OPPOSITION		PLAYED AT	BEVO'S SCORING		
					FG	F	PTS
25.	133	Mountain State	83	Zanesville, OH	27	14	66
26.	102	Beckley	69	Huntington, WV	15	16	46
27.	78	Steubenville	65	Toronto, OH	15	11	41
28.	97	Pikeville	62	Wellsville, OH	24	13	61
29.	126	Mayo State	98	Middleport, OH	24	12	60
30.	104	Cedarville	48	Springfield, OH	18	15	51
31.	116	Mountain State	65	Parkersburg, WV	16	5	37
32.	105	Bliss	69	Wellston, OH	16	17	49
33.	95	Lockbourne Air Force	80	Portsmouth, OH	21	5	47
34.	128	Lees College	57	Chillicothe, OH	22	19	63
35.	100	Wilberforce	51	Cincinnati, OH	21	10	52
36.	128	Bluefield	73	Community Hall	20	13	53
37.	70	Ashland Jr. College	63	Ashland, KY	6	13	25
38.	111	Cincinnati Seminary	86	Gallipolis, OH	22	15	59
39.	109	Wilberforce	55	Cleveland, OH	22	10	54

3,964 Total Points   708   538   1,954

101.6 Average Per Game   18.2   13.8   50.1

1952-53 SEASON BOX SCORES OF OUTSTANDING GAMES

Rio Grande

	G	F	T
Francis	23	23	69
Barr	3	2	8
Gossett	0	0	0
Frasher	0	0	0
Moses	5	2	12
Wiseman	3	2	8
Ripperger	2	2	6
Davis	0	1	1
Renzi	0	1	1
McKenzie	2	2	6
	38	35	111

Wilberforce

	G	F	T
Rutler	12	10	34
Lockett	1	0	2
Gossin	2	6	10
Swanve	3	0	6
Jaune	0	3	3
Jefferson	0	1	1
Fly	2	0	4
Mosely	1	2	4
Chattern	0	0	0
Morris	3	1	7
	24	23	71

Rio Grande

	G	F	T
Francis	27	18	72
Barr	3	6	12
Moses	3	4	10
Wiseman	2	3	7
McKenzie	1	1	3
Viscoglosi	0	1	1
Ripperger	0	0	0
Miller	0	0	0
	36	33	105

California State

	G	F	T
Ruffing	2	0	4
Papini	13	2	28
Johnson	3	4	10
Gorman	2	2	6
Zislinski	5	5	15
Harris	0	2	2
Studnicki	2	2	6
Price	0	2	2
	27	19	73

Rio Grande

	G	F	T
Francis	14	16	44
Barr	4	0	8
Moses	7	3	17
Wiseman	3	4	10
Ripperger	2	1	5
Gossett	1	1	3
Davis	1	2	4
Viscoglosi	0	0	0
	32	27	91

Findlay

	G	F	T
Marquette	8	8	20
Brown	8	6	22
Wolfe	12	3	27
Prince	4	2	10
Rybarezyk	2	0	4
McDowell	0	0	0
Duker	0	1	1
Brooks	1	0	2
Snyder	1	0	2
	36	16	88

Rio Grande

	G	F	T
Barr	3	2	8
Moses	4	5	13
Francis	26	14	66
Wiseman	4	1	9
Viscoglosi	2	1	5
Davis	2	0	4
Gossett	2	0	4
Ripperger	9	2	20
Miller	1	0	2
	53	25	131

Mountain State

	G	F	T
Bibbee	3	2	8
Petty	11	3	25
Ball	6	2	14
Hughes	0	4	4
Southall	3	1	7
Hash	3	3	9
Kelly	5	1	11
Parrish	2	1	5
	33	17	83

Rio Grande

	G	F	T
Francis	20	13	53
Barr	2	2	6
Moses	9	3	21
Ripperger	10	5	25
Wiseman	7	5	19
Mundy	1	0	2
Gossett	1	0	2
	50	28	128

Bluefield

	G	F	T
Jones	2	0	4
Shrader	5	3	13
Savage	2	6	10
Manoskie	9	11	29
Barrow	2	0	4
Jones	3	1	7
Creus	2	0	4
Mitchell	1	0	2
	26	21	73

ONE HUNDRED-SIXTEEN POINTS

The Gallia Times Saturday, January 10, 1953
Game Played - January 9, 1953

Box Score
Rio Grande College

	FG	FT	FA	PF	TP
Francis, c	47	22	29	1	116
Barr, f	2	0	2	5	4
Moses, f	5	2	3	3	12
Wiseman, g	0	3	5	3	3
Ripperger, g	3	2	2	5	8
Gossett, f	1	2	6	5	4
Viscoglosi, f	1	1	3	5	3
Davis, g					
Frasher, g					
Miller, g					
Totals	59	32	50	27	150

Ashland Junior College

	FG	FT	FA	PF	TP
Hobbs, f	9	5	12	4	23
Kennedy, f	3	3	3	4	9
Dingess, c	3	1	1	3	7
Carr, g	0	1	1	5	1
Miller, g	5	6	7	3	16
Slater, f	6	7	13	5	19
Burgess, f	2	4	9	3	8
Oney, c	0	2	2	2	2
Totals	28	29	48	29	85

Quarter Scores	1	2	3	4
Rio Grande College	40	28	27	55
Ashland Jr. College	20	18	18	29

BEVO FRANCIS

6 FT. - 9 IN. CENTER
FROM
RIO GRANDE COLLEGE,
OHIO

HIS FEATS ON THE COURTS
HAVE ATTRACTED NATION-
WIDE ATTENTION

BEVO WENT ON
A SCORING SPREE
LAST SEASON
AND BROKE ALL
EXISTING COLLEGE
RECORDS

IN ONE CONTEST
HE COLLECTED
116 OF THE 150
POINTS SCORED
TO WIN OVER
ASHLAND JR.
COLLEGE

IN THE '52 - '53 SEASON HE
REACHED THE FANTASTIC
NUMBER OF 1,954 POINTS
SCORED IN 39
GAMES

BILL FEVER

Unbeaten through 39 games and seldom extended was this great powerhouse — the 1952-53 Rio Grande College Redmen, rated by experts as the greatest small-college cage power ever assembled.

From left, John Viscoglosi, Jim McKenzie, Wayne Wiseman, Jack Gossett, Bill Frazier, Bevo Francis, Zeke Zempter, Dick Barr, Roy Moses, Bill Ripperger and Bob Mundy.

Student Coach Carroll Kent is at Left-front, along with the old master, Coach Newt Oliver.

Bevo Francis was considered the greatest shooter to have ever played the game of basketball.

During the 1952-53 season he averaged 50.1 points per game with a total point accumulation of 1;954, including a single game high of 116 points.

During his last season at Rio Grande he averaged 47.1, and set the all-time NCAA single game record of 113 points.

Newt Oliver and Bevo Francis are the featured speakers at the B. F. Goodrich Basketball Banquet, held in Akron, Ohio in March of 1953.

THE LAST SEASON:
A DREAM GONE SOUR

When we returned to campus in the fall of 1953, we found the enrollment had increased 42 per cent. One-hundred-twenty-eight students had matriculated. My prediction that interest in Rio Grande would rise came true. Bevo and the other Redmen had been featured in _Life, Look, Newsweek, True, Sport, Real Life, Time,_ and other magazines. We had brought the college a public relations program that one could not put a price on. Even the bad publicity was better than the college was used to—none. In October, President Davis called me into his office and dropped a bombshell. He asked me and Bevo to endorse James Rhodes, Republican candidate for governor of Ohio. I liked and respected Rhodes, but my thinking was that this could only be bad news for Bevo and me. And we were already like hot potatoes in selected circles. I refused Davis' request. The next month, however, we fell into a publicity stunt that would have made a good Hollywood script. Rio Grande is located in Raccoon Township and is subject to its local governance. I noted that no one was on the ballot for township constable, a meaningless office carried over from frontier times. I wrote Bevo Francis' name in when I voted and spent the next several hours campaigning around the village to get others to follow my lead and write Bevo in. Bevo was elected constable and henceforth would reign not only on the basketball court but also in the village. I turned Rhodes down for governor, but I had no hesitation in endorsing Bevo. The news of Bevo's new duties went out to newspapers, radio, and television across the country, The Army newspaper, the _Stars and Stripes,_ featured it in Europe. Bevo soon resigned the office and we got down to the business of basketball.

When Bevo was out of town his wife, Jean Francis took over as Constable of Racoon Township. She is shown here with their son Frank.

Our first game of the second season was an exhibition game at the University of Dayton. The Flyers were ranked fourth nationally. Coach Tom Blackburn's team froze the ball in the last ninety seconds and beat us 63-57. Since your home court is said to be worth an additional twelve points, I felt we could beat Dayton on a neutral court. Blackburn told me after the game on their home court that we were ready for the big time; that we were among the top five teams in the nation. I was ready to go to war against the big teams. We had splendid new uniforms and we were going to fly to games in cities where it was feasible and save the old station wagons for games close by. Keeping a promise to Don Allen, we opened our season against Erie Tech in the Buffalo Memorial Auditorium. The day before we arrived in Buffalo, Dave Garroway's Today show aired a filmed piece on Bevo and Rio Grande. I walked into the magnificent arena. I thought about how just over a year earlier I had told Don Allen that with his help, we would take the Redmen to the big schools. I remembered how my wife and Bevo's had washed team uniforms in a shared bathtub. I thought of our home gym, the Hog Pen, 35' x 80' long. There in that dilapidated building, we often dodged pans of water placed to catch rain coming through the roof as we practiced.

The game with Erie Tech was fast and colorful. Bevo was in top form and, when I took him out of the game with a minute left on the clock, he had sunk twenty-two field goals and twenty of twenty-six free throws. His 64 points that night beat by 22 points the previous record for Memorial Auditorium set the year before by Harry O'Conner of Canasius. The team's 120 topped the previous record of 105 set there in the past by West Texas State. The 5,000 fans who turned out that night gave the Redmen a standing ovation when they left the floor. We were flying now, on commercial aircraft and on the hardwood. I felt I was fronting one of the best basketball teams in the nation. After the Thanksgiving holiday, we prepared to play in New York City's Madison Square Garden. We were the smallest college ever booked there for an athletic contest. Two days before the scheduled game with Adelphi, we drove to Charleston, West Virginia, to board a plane for New York City. Bad weather delayed the take-off and we lost another two hours laying over in Philadelphia waiting for the fog to lift. When we got to our destination we found that every newspaper in the city, except the *Brooklyn Eagle*, was on strike. Ned Irish, the director of Madison Square Garden, was worried about the crowd with the papers shut down. He sent Bevo and me to every radio and television show we could be booked on to give live interviews. Fourteen thousand people turned out to see the Redmen take on Adelphi, a team that had lost to Fordham a few days earlier, 105-56. Adelphi was just a shade better than any good high school team. So here we were in the Garden, a superb basketball team getting ready to take on a weak team. The chance of a lifetime for any coach, any team, any college. We couldn't play a lick. Any group of eighth-grade girls could have taken us out that night. We did lead the

first quarter, 24-19. At the half, we were ahead 43-34, and 60-50 going into the last quarter. They whipped us good, 83-76. Bevo, fighting off three and four players on him all night, got 32 points. Our outside shooting was bad. I worried that self-doubt would now take over the team and Bevo. In fact, I had a hell of a lot of misgivings myself for a while. But I knew enough about life and coaching to know that the measure of an individual and a team is not whether they can handle victory. It is how they handle that inevitable defeat. We had to come back. There was no other choice. When Wiseman hassled me about the game, I told him I never promised that we would win in the Garden. I promised we would play there.

The Redmen's next stop was the Philadelphia Arena where we were scheduled to play Villanova. This would be a severe test to see whether we could make a comeback. No doubt many Philadelphians believed the balloon had burst for us; that the Wildcats would take us down even further. We ended up losing this game by one point in an overtime. Villanova was forced to resort to a high school play to beat us. A player hid behind the referee at midcourt while Bill Ripperger sank two free throws to put us ahead 92-91 with fourteen seconds left. A Villanova player grabbed the ball after the second free throw and threw a full court pass to a player for an easy lay up. Bevo had sent the game into an overtime with a jump shot with twelve seconds left on the clock. This close loss to Villanova gave the Redmen more respect than they had achieved in forty consecutive wins against small colleges. With two losses in a row our invincibility was gone, but it was replaced by the firm conviction that Bevo and Rio Grande were capable of competing against big-league opposition. Eight-thousand fans saw Bevo score 39 points that night on sixteen field goals and seven free throws. Tears flowed after this game, but I told the team it was no disgrace to lose to a team like Villanova. The loss to Adelphi was, however, something else. Our next game was scheduled for the Boston Garden against Providence College, the NIT champion for 1951. Playing before a capacity crowd of 13,000, we had a dogfight from beginning to end. We led 20-18 at the end of the first quarter, trailed at the half 47-43.

Jim McKenzie, one of the great two-handset shot artists in the game of basketball. Playing in a game against Villanova in Philadelphia Arena, he hit four of his first five shots from center court, ending the game with 25 points.

Is He the Greatest?

—By Bob Coyne

THE HIGHLY PUBLICIZED "BEVO" SCORED 1954 POINTS LAST SEASON - INCLUDING 116 ON ASHLAND COLLEGE AND A SPECTACULAR 50 POINT AVERAGE FOR A 39 GAME SCHEDULE

..THE AMAZING "BEVO" AND HIS NEIGHBORHOOD PALS USED TO ADJOURN TO A BARN EVERY FRIDAY AFTERNOON AND PLAY BASKETBALL CONTINUOUSLY UNTIL SUNDAYS DUSK ROLLED AROUND.

..THEY BROUGHT ALONG A THREE DAY SUPPLY OF GRUB AND PASSED THE EVENINGS SLEEPING IN THE HAYLOFT.

IN THE WINGS

BOSTON COLLEGE'S NEW HOOP COACH DON MARTIN AND THE NEW CELTICS STAR JACK NICHOLS WILL MAKE THEIR BOSTON DEBUTS.

CLARENCE "BEVO"
FRANCIS
..THE FABULOUS RIO GRANDE COLLEGE HOOP STAR PERFORMS IN A NOVEL TRIPLE HEADER TOMORROW NIGHT

THE AMAZING 6ft 9in STAR.. CLARENCE **BEVO!** FRANCIS WILL BE ON DISPLAY WHEN HIS RIO GRANDE QUINTET MEETS PROVIDENCE C. AT 7 P.M.

I CAN LICK ANY MAN IN THE HOUSE!

BARKSDALE CELTICS NICHOLS

AT 8:45 THE NEWLY STRENGTHENED CELTICS CLASH WITH MILWAUKEE IN AN N.B.A. ENCOUNTER

IN TONIGHT'S BASKETBALL TRIPLE-HEADER AT THE GARDEN, B.C. TAKES ON ST. ANSELMS AT 5:30 TO START THINGS POPPING!

HOW DO YA DEFEND AGAINST THIS GUY?

2 POINTS! OK! COACH

BEVO SCORED 1954 POINTS LAST SEASON... INCLUDING 116 IN ONE GAME.. AVERAGING A SPECTACULAR 50 POINTS A CONTEST!

LYNN PATRICK LEADS HIS BRUINS AGAINST MONTREAL

EDDIE GERMANO

The third quarter ended with the Redmen ahead 68-67. We won the game 88-87. Bevo, with 41 points, tied the Boston Garden record set by Seattle's Johnny O'Brien the year before. Bevo hit seventeen of thirty-three shots from the floor and twenty of twenty-five free throws.

After beating Providence, we flew back to Charleston, West Virginia. President Davis and an entourage from Rio Grande met us at the airport. Davis asked me how we had done financially. I told him we had cleared at least $10,000. He told me that this money would enable the faculty to receive their pay that month. I was pleased that the team was helping keep the college financially solvent. Our next game was out of the big time against Bluffton College in Bluffton, Ohio, where Kenny Mast was the coach. Ernie Infield, a premier sports writer for the Wooster, Ohio, daily newspaper wrote: "I caught Newt Oliver's protege in action last Friday night when 2,500 fans jammed Bluffton's sparkling new field house to witness another chapter in the fantastic saga of Clarence Francis. Bevo seemed unable to breathe during this game as three Bluffton players dogged him moving out of the pivot. But when his teammates started hitting him with passes, the slaughter was on. The final tally read Rio Grande 116, Bluffton 71. But as far as the fans were concerned, the only points that counted were by Francis." Bevo's scoring by quarters was 17-20-17-28 for a total of 82 points, a new NCAA single-game scoring record. Coach Mast was flabbergasted. He thought his two-man defense, one ahead, one behind, would shackle Bevo. It did not. Mast said he had seen the greatest player the game had ever produced, both amateur and professional. He said that Bevo was the greatest player he had ever seen in action. The next day the Redmen played Hillsdale College in Michigan. The Redmen defeated Hillsdale 82-45 and Bevo's 43 points were within two points of the Hillsdale team. Hillsdale kept the game at a slow pace to hold the scores of Bevo and the team down. At this point in the season, Bevo had 301 points, a 50.2 per game average. The team had won four, lost two, and had outscored its opponents 575-438.

Bevo Francis is pictured with Wayne Wiseman and John Viscoglosi, two of the best college guards in the country.

Real magazine, in the December 1953 issue published a story called, "Bevo Francis: Hot Shot or Hoax?" by Al Helfer, a sportscaster with the Mutual Broadcasting Corporation. Helfer stated that by all odds Bevo was the greatest player in the history of basketball. He predicted that Bevo would prove that fact to everyone before the season was over. He went on to write ". . . that we are seeing in Bevo the most remarkable publicity build up that I have ever known in all the years that I am acquainted with sports. Don't get me wrong, I love Bevo. But Bevo without an astute coach and publicity man named Newt Oliver would be just an agate line in a box score of a little school in Rio Grande, Ohio. Helfer also wrote:

> "For Newt Oliver I predict a tremendous future. He has not yet reached 30 years of age but has the imagination of a Hollywood producer, and technically, he is a first class coach. One must consider him the Svengali to Bevo's Trilby. And he has Bevo liking it. All you need is a coach who is also the publicity director. Then go out and score yourself 116 points in one game and you may be on your way to the big time."

December in the Appalachian Plateau is a bleak time. Dark comes early, the trees are bare, and the weather consists of drizzling rain and a chill air that goes straight to the bones. Once in a while, one would be cheered up by Bing Crosby's song *"White Christmas"* or Patti Page's *"Doggie in the Window."* The Redmen, excited about tales of sunny beaches and babes in Miami, Florida, had one week to prepare for a trip south where they were to play games against three Division One teams in five days. The first game was scheduled against the University of Miami in the Miami Beach Auditorium. It was ironic that Rio Grande, the smallest college in Ohio, would play Miami on a Saturday and the following Monday, the Ohio State University, Ohio's largest university, would take them on. On game night, tickets for the game were scalped for $25. In today's market this would mean $150. Luther Evans, writing for the *Miami Herald*, said that ". . . all Paderewski could do was play the piano and maybe all that storied Bevo Francis can do is shoot, but Lawdy, how that big guy can hit the hoop." When we arrived at the Miami Airport, Don Allen, our sponsor and benefactor, was there to greet us. He had arranged for a ticker tape parade through Miami's Business District. Five new Chevrolet convertibles carried the Redmen entourage escorted by twelve motorcycle policemen. Thousands of people yelled and cheered as we were driven to the Miami City Hall. We were greeted there by the mayor and police chief who made each of us honorary members of the Miami Police Department. An elegant banquet was held in the team's honor. Jim McKenzie, one of the team's guards, said to me, "Coach, this is as close to heaven as you can get and still be on earth."

Going into the deep South in those days of segregation turned out to be a dramatic experience for all of us. We had a black player on the team named Leroy Thompson. When we went to register at the Floridian Hotel, the manager told me that Leroy could not stay there because he was black. I told the manager that we would all stay there or I would take the team to another hotel. The manager reluctantly gave in asking that we have Leroy use the freight elevator. I never told Leroy about it and he rode the same elevator everyone else used. In the game, Leroy took some verbal and physical abuse. I gave the officials hell from the sidelines doing the best I could to keep him safe.

Bevo hit for 48 points, 32 of them in the second half. Before a crowd of 3,521 people, the Redmen beat the Hurricanes 98-88. Near the end of the game, Bevo had an attack of appendicitis and had to be taken from the game. He told a reporter, "I just had to sit down for a while, but when the pain disappeared I asked Coach Oliver to put me back in the game." After the game, Miami's athletic director came into our dressing room and congratulated us. He invited the Redmen for a return contest with an increase in our take of the gate receipts. Ohio State won its game on Monday playing in front of a much smaller crowd. Someone said you could throw a handful of shot into the stand and not touch a spectator at the Ohio State game.

The Redmen's next opponent was North Carolina State University. The Wolfpack was ranked ninth in the nation. On December 21, 1953, we flew from Miami up to Raleigh, North Carolina, for a double-header at the famous Reynolds Coliseum, an arena built from the R. J. Reynolds tobacco fortune. To accommodate smokers, the auditorium had a heating system that circulated fresh air every few minutes. The next two nights of play would determine whether the Redmen would be welcome in the big time or go back to playing bush-league basketball. Back in Gallia County, the *Gallia Times* newspaper ran this headline: "How good is Rio Grande College and scoring sensation Bevo Francis?" Homer Alley, the sports editor, wrote:

> The most difficult question in basketball circles today is just how good is Bevo Francis and his Rio Grande team. If Rio Grande in their game against North Carolina State played up to their potential, and stays within 20 points of their opponent, they will have proven their ability to play in the big time.

The Redmen were scheduled to play the opening game against North Carolina State. Wake Forest was scheduled against the national AAU champions in the second contest. Wake Forest, in its game against the Peoria Caterpillars, faced a team that had won the Olympic title against Argentina in the 1952 games held at Helsinki, Finland. In the Redmen's game against the Wolfpack, Rio Grande was strong in the first half and down two points at the half. I sent our team out in the second half telling them to step up the tempo. It did not work. We missed eight shots straight, fell behind, and lost 77-92! The loss was respectable, but our next opponent, Wake Forest, had defeated N. C. State two weeks earlier 81-69. Seventy-five-hundred fans were on hand as we controlled the tipoff and led at the quarter 19-12. At the half, Wake led 35-30. Going into the last quarter we were behind one point, 49-50. In the melee of the last quarter, Wake led 60-59 with less than three minutes left on the clock. The crowd began booing the Deacons as they missed five straight free throws. With a minute left to play, Wiseman stole the ball and passed to Ripperger who flipped one in to tie the game at sixty-five. With five seconds left and in possession of the ball, I called a time-out. I wanted the last shot of the game in regulation to be by the greatest scorer to have ever played the game, Bevo Francis. The game's outcome was his burden. The ball was put in play near the center of the court. Dick Barr passed to Ripperger, who lobbed it off to Bevo. Two seconds were left when Bevo ran from under the basket to the free throw line. It was the prettiest shot I ever saw. The ball hit the net, the game was over. Rio Grande, the little school from the sticks with sixty male students, defeated the team that had defeated the 1952 Olympic champions the night before.

The Redmen and I flew back home a happy, unified team. We had been on the road since December 16th. It was Christmas Eve, and I rushed to the post office to pick up the mail. I ran into one of our strongest supporters at the post office, Findley Richards. He lived next door to President Davis and when he told me he needed to tell me something, I listened carefully. He told me Davis had been saying that one way or the other he was going to get rid of me and the team when the season was over. I was not surprised. I gathered up a large bag of mail with post marks from all over the United States and foreign countries. I knew, however, that trouble was brewing and pondered how to handle my side of the problem. I will admit I never had much training in conflict resolution and never received an award for diplomacy.

Early in the new year, 1954, the team came back to campus after celebrating the holidays. We loaded up and headed for Parkersburg, West Virginia, for a game against Salem College. In the first few minutes of this game, I called a time-out and one of our players remarked that there was no way we would beat Salem against biased officials. I conceded the point telling him we will get them next time. They beat us 99-96. I had made the mistake when contracts were initiated of not demanding that one of the officials at away games be named by Rio Grande. When the Redmen played Salem a few weeks later in the Huntington Field House, we beat them 115-76, a spread of thirty-nine points. We had proved our point.

We moved quickly back to the major leagues. It was on to Indianapolis, Indiana, to play Butler University, the 1929 NCAA national champions. The Butler Fieldhouse was filled to capacity with 11,593 paid admissions, an attendance record. The skeptical Hoosiers turned out to see a legend debunked but, instead, saw history made. With 48 points, Bevo broke the Fieldhouse scoring record set a month earlier by Paul Ebert of Ohio State with 34. Just a year earlier Ohio State's coach, Floyd Stahl, had said he had to be careful in saying anything derogatory about Bevo as he used his influence to rein in the Redmen. To see his player's record fall to Bevo was sweet revenge. Angelo Agelopolous wrote in the *Indianapolis News* that ". . basketball coaches always dwell at length on systems, plays and patterns, and then will, in a burst of confessions, admit that actually what the game breaks down to is getting the ball in the basket, and that Bevo Francis has reduced basketball to its simplest form." Jep Cadow, Jr., *Indianapolis Star* sports editor, said that Bevo and his teammates had written one of the brightest chapters in Butler Field House history. He called Bevo the 6'9" coon hunter from Rio Grande. Angelopolous described the game this way: "At the quarter, it was Rio Grande 24, Butler 13, Bevo 13; at the half, Rio Grande 43, Butler 27, Bevo 27; at the third quarter, Rio Grande 58, Butler 44, Bevo 36. The entire Butler team had begun to outscore him after three quarters. The final score was 81-68." Bevo received a standing ovation for breaking the field house record. When we got back to Rio Grande the next day, Dave Garroway's television crew was waiting to make a six-minute film review to show on the *Today* show. This film gave the college one-hundred-dred-eighty-thousand dollars worth of free publicity. Still, in spite of our accomplishments, the team and I felt resentment by the administration and selected faculty members. We were told that the tail was wagging the dog. The truth of the matter was, we were feeding the dog and helping it stay alive financially.

The Redmen's next game was against Morris Harvey in Charleston, West Virginia. Wayne Wiseman took over the spotlight. In the last quarter, the team moved into its fancy ball handling routine. Wiseman made a behind-the-back pass the length of the court. Bevo caught the ball and turned it into a fast basket as the crowd gave Wiseman a standing ovation. We were at our peak, idolized from coast to coast. On campus, however, we were held in contempt. A sports writer for a West

THE FABULOUS "BEVO"
IN HIS ONLY LOCAL
APPEARANCE OF THE
SEASON AT THE
CINCINNATI GARDEN, TONIGHT

Virginia paper said that the team acted and played more like professionals than college players. In fact, we were professionals bringing in money to pay the faculty and other college bills. The following week the Redmen played Alliance College in the Gannon Auditorium in Erie, Pennsylvania. Wes Driscol, a sports writer, said that Wayne Wiseman was the only player in the history of the Gannon arena to get a standing ovation from the crowd without making one field goal. He dribbled and passed beyond our wildest dreams. When I took him out of the game and the fans knew he was through for the night, the roar went up. Another writer wrote that Constable Francis of Racoon Township in Ohio has not arrested anyone yet and has never drawn his shooting iron. But as a basketball whiz from Rio Grande, he arrests his opponents with ease. He scored 61 points, often leading the team's fast breaks as the Redmen won 107-77 before 2,600 spectators. Tom Macguire, writing for an Erie newspaper, stated that both Bevo's and the Redmen's totals were auditorium records, and that on occasion his teammates passed up good shots of their own to get the ball to Bevo so that his average stayed beyond the reach of opposing players. The next night the Redmen went back to Bevo's hometown of Wellsville to play our second game with Alliance College. The 131 points the Redmen scored was the high mark of the season. Bevo sunk thirty-seven field goals and eight free-throws. These 84 points set a new NCAA record for a single game. The twenty-one year-old, 6' 9" center boosted his scoring for the season to 688 points in fourteen games, averaging 50 points per game.

The Redmen's fifteenth game was scheduled in the Washington Gymnasium in Gallipolis, Ohio. The game was played for the benefit of the 1954 March of Dimes campaign. Having raised thousands of dollars for the fight against polio, we were heralded as the March of Dimes team. We were playing Ashland college of Ohio, a team I felt would be a pushover. Bevo played all but two minutes of the contest pumping in twenty-two field goals and eleven of twelve free-throws. Seven hundred people crowded into the small gym shelling out $2.25 and $4.25 per seat. This would compare to $13.50 and $25.50 tickets at today's prices. Hundreds of fans were turned away. During the first half, Bevo could not find the range as he scored only sixteen points. However, he rang up another thirty-nine in the second half for a total of 55 before a roaring crowd. The Redmen hit 56 per cent of their field goals and twenty-nine of thirty-six free throws.

Si Burick, sports editor of the _Dayton Daily News_ and a friend of Don Allen, visited me at Rio Grande inquiring about our playing a March of Dimes benefit in Dayton. He asked what we would expect for a guarantee. I told him to make us an offer. He opened with $500.00. I asked for $5,000. Silence. Then Si said, "There is no use having a polio benefit if only Rio Grande College is benefited." I asked Burick to walk out of my office, turn left, and look at our gym floor. There were pots and pans scattered around the floor to catch rain that came in and the college had no money to replace the roof. He came back smiling. We settled on $4,000 and I signed up to play Findlay College. Everybody won. Forty-four thousand dollars were taken in from the game. Four-thousand people turned out screaming and hollering as Findlay's Ron Marquette outscored Bevo with 36 points. The Redmen won 74-71 even though Bevo's 32 was the second time he was outscored in a college game. The next night the Redmen played Creighton University at the Arena in Troy, Ohio. Creighton's strategy was to foul Bevo before he could get a shot off. As soon as he got the ball, he was fouled sending him to the free-throw line. At that time, a player got one free throw unless he was getting off a shot. He was fouled fourteen times in a row but managed to score 49 points. The Redmen won 96-90. Now facing Morris Harvey of West Virginia in the Cincinnati Garden, I tried to get the game postponed because Bevo had the flu. The Garden officials did not want to postpone so we went on. Bevo was weak but said he could play. We won the game 74-61 before 6,000 fans with Bevo scoring only 26. Four days later, the Redmen traveled to Buffalo, New York, to play Buffalo State. Four thousand people greeted the team with a standing ovation when they took the floor at the Connecticut Street armory. Bevo was short with 31 points as the Redmen won 81-65.

Bevo's average had dropped to 46.3, but a game was forthcoming that would be heard around the world, and Bevo Francis' name would become immortal in the history of basketball.

On February 2, 1954, the Redmen were scheduled against Hillsdale College of Michigan, the second round of a home and home. The game was played in Jackson, Ohio, in the high school gym. In practice for this game, I stressed an aggressive style of defense. We were going to press them for forty minutes. In the Redmen's first game against Hillsdale, they used every tactic available to slow the game. At the half, Bevo had 43 points. I had a sense that this could become the mother of all games for an individual to set an individual scoring record. Ever since the NCAA had Bevo's 116 points against Ashland thrown out, I had waited for this chance. Bevo had 74 points at the beginning of the fourth quarter. I knew that he could reach 100 in the ten minutes of play left. Bevo was 26 points away from tying Frank Selvy's record 100 points when Furman University played Newberry College. In the last quarter, Bevo scored 39 points for a game total of 113. The Associated Press reported that the fabulous Bevo Francis scored 113 points last night as his Rio Grande basketball team walloped Hillsdale College 134-91. Newspapers, radio, and television from coast to coast had banner headlines announcing that Bevo had reclaimed his national one-game scoring record. Bevo's free throws totaled thirty-seven out of forty-two attempted, a national record for one game. These records stand today, forty-two years after the fact. The college board of trustees' president, J. Boyd Davis, had his picture taken with Bevo in Community Hall and announced that Rio Grande had received over $100,000 in gifts from alumni and friends, one-third of their three-year fund drive goal. A good fund raiser could have turned this event into at least a million dollars. In spite of the Redmen's overwhelming success, I could sense that our days were numbered at Rio Grande. President Davis and Dean W. A. Lewis continued to complain that Rio Grande's traditional values were incongruent with the attention the Redmen were getting.

Bevo Francis shoots and scores against Hillsdale College on February 2, 1954, in Jackson, Ohio. He ended the game with 113 points, the all-time NCAA single game record.

Even though Hillsdale College placed a three-man blitz around the fabulous Bevo Francis, the Rio Grande College ace scored 113 points in this game played on Feb. 2, 1954 at Jackson, Ohio. No. 19 for The Redmen is Dick Myers, No. 22 Don Vynalek, No. 26 Lee Weir and No. 29 Al Schreiber.

Newt Oliver holds the ball that Bevo Francis used in scoring 113 points against Hillsdale College of Michigan, the All-time NCAA single game record. The ball was donated to the Basketball Hall of Fame, Springfield, Massachusetts, where it is now on display.

The Redmen moved on to Anderson, Indiana, to play Anderson College. Hundreds of fans were turned away from the gym that was filled to capacity with 4,600 people. Bevo scored 59 points as Rio Grande won 101-85. In the fourth quarter on a free throw, Bevo broke the NCAA record for a season. His total for the year of 988 eclipsed the old mark of 970 set at Seattle University by Johnny O'Brien in 1951-52. He also set a new record for the Anderson auditorium beating Johnny Wilson's forty-nine points. Wilson later played for the Harlem Globetrotters. A nearby city newspaper covered our next contest at Ashland College, Ashland, Ohio, and following is the writer's view of that contest:

> At long last we have taken our place among the fortunate who have watched Bevo Francis and his Rio Grande playmates in action. The Red-men defeated Ashland 121-81. Bevo got 54 points against the Eagles. But Ashland College has disgraced itself in athletic competition. Never have we seen a basketball player take the brutal pounding the brilliant Mr. Francis took last night. A lot of games have been called "dirty," but this one took its place well up on the list.

Sixty-nine personal fouls were called during the game. This game should have ended our season. Bevo sprained an ankle and was examined at nearby Mansfield General Hospital for a possible fracture. Bevo now had accumulated 1,171 points and his average was 50-plus. The Redmen had two games left, which I tried to postpone. Bevo was limping and I wanted time for his ankle to heal and time to keep his average above fifty.

The manager of the Cleveland Arena offered Rio Grande $5,000 to play in a four-team elimination tournament. The winner would advance to the NAIA national tournament in Kansas City. The team and I left for Cleveland in two station wagons. We got as far as Mansfield when a deep snow forced us to take a train for the remainder of the trip. The first round

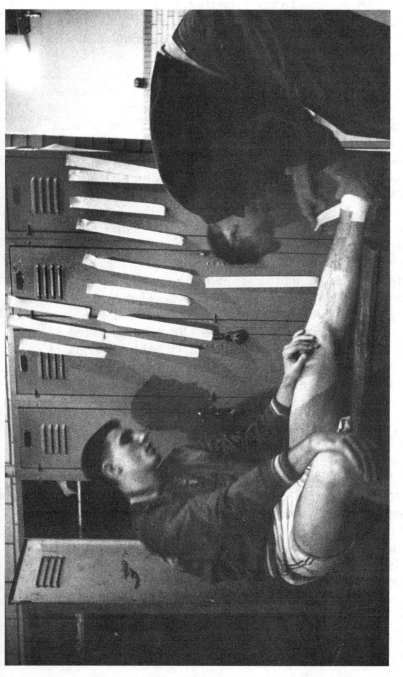

Coach Newt Oliver tapes the sprained ankle of Bevo Francis. This injury caused his average to drop from 50.6 to 47.1 points during the last four games of the 1953-54 season.

of the NAIA district cage playoffs was to feature George Dalton of John Carroll College and Herk Wolf from Findlay College. The Redmen's opponent was to be Central State. The snow continued to fall, closing down all modes of travel including the airport. The games were cancelled and Rio Grande was out its $5,000 guarantee. When the weather cleared up and we got back to Rio Grande, an offer to play in the national NAIA tournament was offered to the Redmen. There was not enough time for another elimination tournament. Rio Grande was seeded first in a field of thirty-two teams. In the first game against Arizona State the Redmen won 90-74. Bevo, playing on an injured ankle, scored 28 points as the largest opening-night crowd, 10,500, in the history of the tournament turned out. The next night the Redmen lost to Southeastern Louisiana 78-65. Bevo scored a little more than half his average, 27. The Redmen, however, made a major contribution to the tournament with their ability to draw a crowd. The Redmen moved on to a rescheduled game in the St. Louis Arena against Shurtleff College of Alton, Illinois, a team whose record was 20-3. Bevo, still limping, scored 37 points in a contest the team won 72-70. I told Maury White of the *Omaha Daily News* that we were about thirty points worse than we were at the peak of the season. Bevo's injured ankle was a large contributing factor to our slide into mediocrity.

During our two years at Rio Grande we raised thousands of dollars for the fight against polio. Now we were given a chance to raise funds for the Shriner's Hospital for Crippled Children in Kansas City. The Redmen were invited to play at the third annual East-West All-Star contest. Stanley Garity, Potentate of the Ararat Temple, stated in the *Kansas City Star* that the signing of Rio Grande and its highly publicized star would mean a sellout game in the auditorium. After I agreed to play there, Garrity told me that Dr. Bland Standley of the Ohio State University was trying to keep the Redmen out of the game. Garrity assured me that he would see that we got to play. Playing in the next-to-last game in which he would wear the Rio Grande College colors of red, white, and blue, Bevo was still nursing his ankle injury. In the Redmen's game against Rockhurst College, the officiating, reminiscent of a previous effort against Ashland College, was out of control. Rockhurst was ahead 56-50 with two minutes left on the clock when one of the Redmen sustained a flagrant foul. I took the team off the floor and forfeited the game. As we left the floor during a standing ovation, Adolph Rupp, basketball coach at the University of Kentucky, came into our dressing room and asked me if the officials were changed would we finish the game? I told Rupp as far as I was concerned the game was over. He said he did not blame me for taking the team out under the circumstances. The Redmen's final game was played against Creighton University in Omaha, Nebraska. The game was played at Boy's Town gym, the largest arena in the Omaha area. A sellout crowd of 6,500 came to see the game. The gym was so crowded that the team and I had to sit among the fans. The Redmen lost 93-75. Bevo scored 41 points in his last college game.

The Redmen ended the season with a record of 21-7. Bevo scored 1,318 points, averaging 47.1 per game. Bevo's ankle injury was a big negative in the team's last five games. The team played in front of over 169,000 people in some of the biggest arenas in the country. We made personal appearances on a routine basis. We climbed the ladder against odds that staggered the imagination. The Redmen were an inspiration to small college basketball players everywhere. Hundreds of letters flooded my office requesting autographs and information about Bevo and the team. Ned Irish of the Madison Square Garden sent me a contract for the next season with a $5,000 guarantee. A disclaimer in the contract was: No Bevo, no game. The manager of the Houston Coliseum offered us a $7,000 guarantee, the largest ever offered in Texas history. This guarantee would equal $42,000 in today's money. The Coliseum seated 12,000 people.

Late March came and the resentment of the team by Rio Grande administrators and some faculty members continued. Bevo walked into my office one afternoon and told me that his debts were piling up and he was going to quit school and go

97

Against many of the top-ranked major cage powers in the country, this 1953-54 edition of the Rio Grande College Redmen posted an impressive 21-7 record.

From left to right, Coach Newt Oliver, Al Schreiber, Jim McKenzie, Wayne Wiseman, Dick Myers, Dick Barr, Bevo Francis, Jack Gossett, Bernie Lipkofer, Don Vynalek, Roy Moses, Bill Ripperger and Carroll Kent, student coach.

to work. President Davis had turned him down for a small loan to buy groceries and some faculty members remained aloof and indifferent. In his two years at Rio Grande, he was never tutored by a private tutor. His grades were above the academic requirement for probation. He had no F's on his record. The next day, he and his wife Jean loaded up their car and headed back to Wellsville. The party was over. In spite of the fact that Bevo withdrew properly from the college two weeks earlier, a committee comprised of three professors and Dean W. A. Lewis told the Associated Press that Bevo had been expelled. Shabby treatment if I ever saw it. The team and Bevo were expendable even though money was coming in as never before. Larry Donald, editor of *Basketball Times* wrote:

> But, like it or not, the record will show that Rio Grande used up its student-athlete for fun and profit, then tossed him unceremoniously out. And as for Newt Oliver: Looking back no one can argue that his short, turbulent coaching tenure is the largest single reason the college exists today.

During the 1953-54 season, Bevo scored more than half of the Redmen's points. The team scored 2,556 while Bevo scored 1,318. This was a first in the sport of basketball, and it has not happened since. Success often brings about contempt, especially when one's ability exceeds that of people who are out of the picture. I was continually criticized by college officials for making mistakes. But some mistakes were inevitable in bringing about a successful program in such a short period of time at a school where mediocrity was the normal routine in athletics. But if I had run my personal affairs over the years the way Rio Grande College was run in those years I would be on welfare. When the All-American teams were announced, Bevo made the second team. This was the first and only time a player from a college as small as Rio Grande ever reached that height. The last five games of the season may have kept Bevo off the first team. It was now time to look toward new horizons.

Don Allen offered me the following deal, his words: "Come with my organization as public relations director and I will lay a blank check on the table. You can fill in the blanks." But I could still see the stars and hear the applause of thousands of basketball fans. I could still smell the popcorn and the sweaty locker rooms. I turned him down. This was a big mistake. A bigger one was just days away. I had been in contact for several days with Abe Saperstein, the head of the Harlem Globetrotters. I flew to New York City and entered into negotiations for a contract that would bring Bevo and me into their organization. After two days of discussion, Bevo and I signed on to perform a sideshow for the Globetrotters. I was to coach Bevo and the Boston Whirlwinds for 130 games against the Globetrotters on makeshift courts from coast to coast. We understood that Bevo would be allowed to play with limited physical contact. Instead, he took physical punishment game after game, uncalled for since this was exhibition basketball. It got so bad during the summer of 1954 that we both nearly quit. Finally, we complained to Saperstein and he agreed to order the opposition teams to take it easy on Bevo. I realized then that we should have taken another direction. We would have been better off if we had formed our own barnstorming team and toured the United States. We would have made more money and retained control of our destiny. Several million dollars was easily possible. Instead, we were working for $20,000, $12,000 for Bevo and $8,000 for me. I have always heard that opportunity knocks once and the second time it's the house detective. This was, in a light-hearted way, the way it was. I have a deep sense of regret that I led Bevo into signing with the Globetrotters. He looked to me for proper guidance in turning professional and, in that respect, I failed.

My contract was:

AGREEMENT

This agreement made and entered into this 26th. day of April A.D. 1954 by and between A. M. Saperstein of Chicago, Illinois, Party of the First Part, Herein-after referred to as "Saperstein" and Newt

Oliver, of Rio Grande, Ohio, Party of the Second Part, Hereinafter referred to as "Oliver."

WITNESSETH

Whereas, Saperstein is the owner and manager of several athletic teams, and

Whereas, Oliver is a basketball coach, and

Whereas, Saperstein desires to employ Oliver and Oliver desires to accept said employment.

Now, therefore, it is agreed by and between the parties hereto as follows:

1. Saperstein engages Oliver to render services as a basketball coach and trainer upon the terms herein-after set forth and Oliver agrees to accept such employment upon the following terms.

2. The term of employment shall commence on the First day of October, 1954, and shall continue until the Thirtieth day of September, 1955, and thereafter as provided further herein.

3. Saperstein agrees to pay Oliver and Oliver agrees to accept, the sum of eight thousand dollars ($8,000.00) and to further pay the traveling expenses of the said Oliver and to provide Oliver with lodging when his duties require him to be absent from his home in Rio Grande, Ohio.

4. Oliver agrees that during the period of employment, he will devote his full time and attention to the performance of his duties.

5. Oliver agrees to coach and train basketball players as directed by Saperstein and to act, if so directed, as traveling secretary and manager of any of the athletic teams operated by Saperstein.

6. Oliver agrees to so conduct himself as not to injure his good reputation or the reputation of the athletic organizations of Saperstein.

101

7. This contract shall be renewed with all the conditions and agreements on the part of both parties to be kept and performed for one year from October 1, 1955, to September 30, 1956, if Saperstein desires to renew said contract and notifies Oliver that he intends to so renew on or before the 1st day of September, 1955. Such notice shall be sufficient if sent by Saperstein by mail to the last and usual place of abode of Oliver known to Saperstein.

8. Oliver shall make no personal appearances nor endorce any commercial product or appear in any motion pictures or television shows and radio broadcasts without the written consent of Saperstein or upon his direction. Oliver agrees to appear in such motion pictures, television shows, and radio broadcasts as Saperstein may direct and which shall have as their purpose the publicizing of Saperstein's athletic organizations or of Oliver.

9. Should any provisions of this contract be hereinafter determined to be invalid, such determination shall not invalidate the other provisions contained herein.

10. This agreement shall be construed to have been made under, and shall be governed by, the laws of the state of Illinois.

In witness whereof, the parties hereto have here-unto set their hands and seals the day and year first above written.

A. M. Saperstein

Newt Oliver
April 26, 1954

Accession to agreement entered into between A. M. Saperstein, hereinafter called the party of the first part, and Newt Oliver and Clarence "Bevo" Francis.

The party of the first part herein agrees to consider the relationship between Newt Oliver and Clarence "Bevo" Francis as a joint one, and it will remain as such during the tenure of the agreement herein entered into.

(In every city we visited with the Globetrotters, we got more billing than they did. We traveled from city to city like a circus playing one-night stands on a portable basketball court in lighted baseball parks. Among the players on the tour were George Mikan, Bob Davies, Goose Tatum, Bill Spivey, Sweetwater Clifton, and Walter Dukes. Our first game was at the

Two of basketball's most-colorful promoters, the late and great Abe Saperstein, left, and Newt Oliver, center, pour approximately 4,000 one dollar bills on table, which represented a down payment paid to Oliver and his great star, Bevo Francis, right, for signing a Harlem Globetrotter contract.

104

Miami Stadium on June 24, 1954, and we ended the tour on August, 30 in Springfield, Illinois. We played fifty-seven games. In September we went into training in Chicago preparing for the winter tour. In the 1950s there were three Harlem Globetrotter units playing in three sections of the country. We were assigned to the western unit which played in North Dakota, South Dakota, Montana, Wyoming, and other states. This was the boondocks section. Bevo and I thought we would play in the eastern unit which performed in major cities. Fans in these major arenas were clamoring to see Bevo and managers there were asking for him. Saperstein later apologized to us for the assignment. We were able to play in a few major arenas in Seattle, Vancouver, and Spokane. We earned our season pay in these three cities alone. In Vancouver, Canada, we drew two of the largest crowds in the history of the University of British Columbia War Memorial Field House. In Spokane, Washington, we set a new attendance record of 7,355 in the Spokane Coliseum. The travel and experiences were educational. Both later proved to be a great asset in teaching high school students about the United States. But living out of a suitcase is a tough way to make a living. Even carnival workers spend four or five days in one place. The Globetrotters always played one-night stands. When we ended our first winter tour in Jackson, Michigan, we had played 135 games. When I finally got back to Rio Grande, my wife said she wanted to move to Springfield, Ohio, so she could be near her relatives while I was on tour. In the summer of 1955 we were assigned to the eastern unit. Goose Tatum, the Globetrotter super star, had quit to form his own team. Meadowlark Lemon was groomed to replace Tatum as the primary clown. But there was only one Goose, and Meadowlark never measured up to Tatum as the clown prince of basketball. Lemon was funny but Goose was just a natural clown. Marcus Haynes, the greatest basketball dribbler of all time, also quit the Globetrotters bringing their luster even further down. Sweetwater Clifton was sold to the New York Nicks. Three legendary figures were now gone their separate ways. Formed in 1927 by Abe Saperstein, this team was originally called the Savoy Big Five, then

105

Newt Oliver's Frostop Drive-In Restaurant in Springfield, Ohio, 1965. Selling an average of 25,000 gallons of Root Beer per season, it was the most popular Drive-In in the city.

the New York Globetrotters and, finally, the Harlem Globetrotters. After two-and-a-half years of coaching and public relations with the Trotters, I was pretty much ready to move on. My last assignment was as a public relations director on the Trotters College All-American team. This annual tour pitted the senior members of the college All-American team against the best of the three Globetrotter teams. At the end of this tour I turned down a permanent position as their director of public relations. My days with the Globetrotters were over.

In the spring of 1956, I accepted a teaching job in a consolidated high school in Clark County, Ohio, known as Northwestern High School. Three years later, my wife and I started a drive-in restaurant and root beer stand on the edge of Springfield. We sold root beer in glasses letting the customers keep the glass as a souvenir. We averaged 25,000 gallons of root beer each summer. Continuing to teach until 1964, I worked summers at the restaurant from 9:00 a.m. to 11:00 p.m. seven days a week. In the spring of 1972, we sold the restaurant and, at age forty-seven, I retired. In 1979, I ran successfully for Clark County Commissioner and served two four-year terms.

Bevo Francis quit the Globetrotters and played basketball in the Eastern Professional League. He was drafted by Philadelphia of the National Basketball Association. In those days the money was limited, and he turned them down. He continued to play for a variety of industrial teams until 1962 when he retired from sports. Bevo retired last year from the Akron Goodyear Corporation. He lives in the village of Highlandtown in eastern Ohio spending much time with his grandchildren. He still hunts and fishes, a family man in every respect. He is a hero to many young athletes and Rio Grande College honors him annually at the Bevo Classic basketball tournament.

Wayne Wiseman, after two years in the Army, became a high school basketball coach. He coached at Oak Hill in Jackson County and, later, Northwestern and Springfield South high schools. He is now retired.

Dick Barr transferred from Rio Grande to Findlay College where he played out his two remaining years of eligibility. He graduated in 1956. From Findlay, Barr worked for the Goodyear Rubber Company in Akron and played amateur ball in the National Industrial League. He is still with the company as field representative living in North Canton, Ohio.

Roy Moses, sometimes called "professor" by his teammates because of his academic skills in chemistry and physics, retired as a physics teacher in the Oak Hill School district near Thurman, Ohio, where he lives.

Bill Ripperger coached at Anna and, later, at Botken High School in Shelby County, Ohio. His last teaching and coaching job was at Norwood High School, his alma mater, in Cincinnati, Ohio. He died in 1978 at age 45.

Jim McKenzie retired several years ago as basketball coach and athletic director at Symmes Valley High School. This consolidated district was once the home of the famous Waterloo Wonders. He was the last of the great two-handed set shots. In the Villanova game, he made four of his first five shots from the center of the court.

John Viscoglosi, drafted into the Army while still a member of the undefeated 1952-53 team, retired from a local steel mill in East Liverpool, Ohio, where he lives. At Rio Grande he was known as the Wellsville flash.

Don Vyhnalek transferred to Doane College in Crete, Nebraska, where he made the Little All-American team. He is a supervisor in the product claims division of the Ford Motor Company in Dearborn, Michigan.

In June 1995, Bevo and I signed contracts with the Disney Movie Studio giving them the rights to film the story of the famous Redmen team. Epitaphs and eulogies for this team are not appropriate. As long as basketball is discussed across America, the Rio Grande College legend will live on. Legends never go out of style.

1953-54 ROSTER

Clarence "Bevo" Francis	6'9"	Hammondsville, Ohio	Sophomore
Wayne "Wonder" Wiseman	6"	Waterloo, Ohio	Senior
Bill "Shotgun" Ripperger	6'	Norwood, Ohio	Senior
Roy "Bull" Moses	6'1"	Upper Sandusky, Ohio	Junior
Dick "Cheta" Barr	6'2"	Ashland, Ohio	Sophomore
Jim McKenzie	5'10"	Cattlettsburg, Kentucky	Sophomore
Richard "Dick" Myers	6'3"	Coal Grove, Ohio	Freshman
Leroy "Cat" Thompson	6'1"	Waynesburg, Ohio	Freshman
Don Vyhnalek	6'3"	Crete, Nebraska	Freshman
Robert Zurcher	6'3"	Minerva, Ohio	Freshman
Lee Weiher	5'9"	Rio Grande, Ohio	Freshman
Al Schreiber	5'9"	New York, NY	Sophomore

PLAYERS WHO TURNED PROFESSIONAL

Bevo Francis

Wayne Wiseman

Bill Ripperger

Al Schreiber

Jim McKenzie

AP
ALL-AMERICAN TEAMS
1954

FIRST TEAM

Player	School	Total Points	First Team Points
Frank Selvy	Furman	1,482	280
Don Schlundt	Indiana	1,209	209
Tom Gola	LaSalle	1,146	202
Cliff Hagan	Kentucky	1,101	193
Bob Petit	Louisiana State	784	102

SECOND TEAM

Player	School	Total Points	First Team Points
Bevo Francis	Rio Grande	767	119
Bob Leonard	Indiana	595	93
Frank Ramsey	Kentucky	580	82
Dick Ricketts	Duquesne	496	70
Tom Marshall	West Kentucky	406	51

THE LAST SEASON

	Rio	Opposition		Played At	Bevo's
1.	120	Erie Tech.	59	Buffalo, NY	64
2.	76	Adelphi	83	Madison Square Garden	32
3.	92	Villanova	93	Philadelphia, PA	39
4.	89	Providence	87	Boston, MA	41
5.	116	Bluffton	71	Bluffton, OH	82
6.	82	Hillsdale	45	Hillsdale, MI	43
7.	98	Miami University	88	Miami, FL	48
8.	77	North Carolina State	92	Raleigh, NC	34
9.	67	Wake Forest	65	Raleigh, NC	32
10.	96	Salem	99	Clarksburg, WV	38
11.	81	Butler	68	Indianapolis, IN	48
12.	86	Morris Harvey	63	Charleston, WV	41
13.	107	Alliance College	77	Erie, PA	61
14.	133	Alliance College	68	Wellsville, OH	84
15.	117	Ashland College	74	Gallipolis, OH	55
16.	74	Findlay	71	Dayton, OH	32
17.	96	Creighton University	90	Troy, OH	49
18.	74	Morris Harvey	62	Cincinnati, OH	26
19.	81	Buffalo State	65	Buffalo, NY	31
20.	134	Hillsdale	91	Jackson, OH	113
21.	101	Anderson	85	Anderson, IN	59
22.	115	Salem	76	Huntington, WV	58
23.	121	Ashland	61	Ashland, OH	53
24.	90	Arizona State	74	Kansas City, MO	28
25.	65	S.E. Louisiana	78	Kansas City, MO	27
26.	73	Shurtleff	72	St. Louis, MO	37
27.	50	Rockhurst	56	Kansas City, MO	22
28.	75	Creighton University	93	Omaha, NE	41
	2,585	Total Points	2,126		1,318

Average Per Game   92.3
Opponent's Average Per Game   75.7
Bevo's Average   47.1
Attendance   164,000

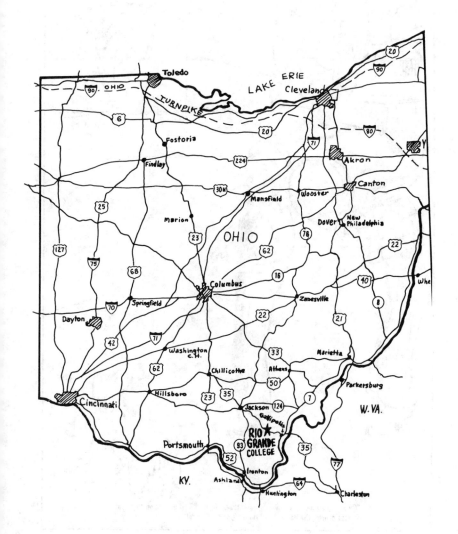

"By saving my money and playing basketball, I figure I'll be able to go to a real famous college, like Harvard, or Princeton, or Rio Grande!"

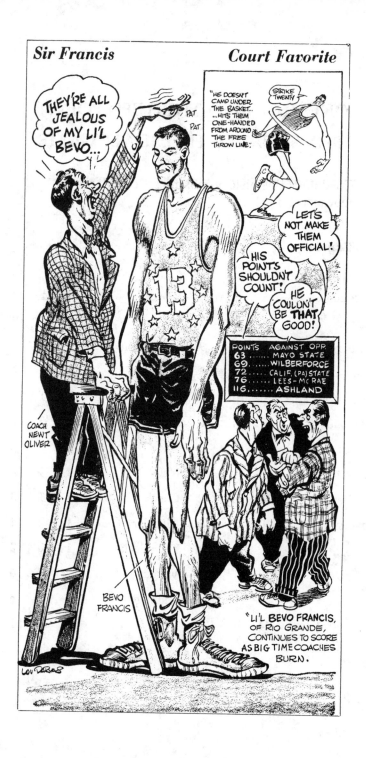

ONE HUNDRED-THIRTEEN POINTS
BOX SCORE OF HILLSDALE GAME

The date of this history-making spectacular was February 2, 1954.

Rio Grande	G	F	T	Hillsdale	G	F	T
Wiseman	1	2	4	Lowry	4	1	9
Barr	1	0	2	Helsted	6	7	19
Ripperger	2	5	9	Kincannon	0	3	3
Francis	38	37	113	Wagner	1	0	2
McKenzie	0	0	0	Davis	7	11	25
Vyhnalek	0	0	0	Sewell	0	3	3
Moses	1	0	2	Fake	0	2	2
Gossett	0	1	1	Neff	4	4	12
Weiher	1	0	2	Check	1	1	3
Myers	0	1	1	Allinder	1	2	4
				Thiendeck	1	0	2
				Vushan	2	0	4
				Tallmen	1	1	3
Totals	44	46	134		28	35	91

1953-54 SEASON

BOX SCORES OF OUTSTANDING GAMES

Rio Grande

	G	F	T
McKenzie	6	1	13
Ripperger	2	0	4
Francis	28	5	61
Wiseman	0	2	2
Barr	8	0	16
Vyhnalek	2	4	8
Gossett	1	1	3
Totals	47	13	107

Alliance College

	G	F	T
Czackowski	3	1	7
Minichelli	2	6	10
Kaliszak	10	4	24
Maslowski	5	1	11
Czenis	7	5	19
Ryzowkz	1	2	4
Kraemer	1	0	2
	29	19	77

Rio Grande

	G	F	T
Barr	2	0	4
Gossett	1	1	3
Ripperger	3	0	6
Moses	3	2	8
Francis	38	8	84
Myers	1	0	2
McKenzie	1	0	2
Vyhnalek	6	1	13
Wiseman	5	1	11
Totals	60	13	133

Alliance College

	G	F	T
Czackowski	3	3	9
Minichelli	3	3	9
Kaliszak	3	2	8
Maslowski	8	5	21
Czenis	6	7	19
Ryzowkz	1	0	2
Kraemer	0	2	2
	24	22	70

Rio Grande

	G	F	T
McKenzie	5	1	11
Vyhnalek	1	0	2
Ripperger	3	0	6
Francis	12	8	32
Wiseman	6	1	13
Moses	0	1	1
Barr	1	0	2
Totals	28	11	67

Wake Forest

	G	F	T
Deporter	6	1	13
Davis	4	3	11
George	3	0	6
Hemric	9	6	24
Lyles	1	1	3
Lipstas	3	2	8
	26	13	65

Rio Grande

	G	F	T
Wiseman	1	8	10
Barr	3	2	8
Francis	17	14	48
Ripperger	0	0	0
McKenzie	4	2	10
Vyhnalek	2	1	5
Moses	0	0	0
Totals	27	27	81

Butler

	G	F	T
Greve	8	6	22
Reed	1	1	3
Labads	0	0	0
Mustain	1	1	3
MacKenzie	4	0	8
Crosley	6	6	18
Ellenberger	5	0	10
Porter	0	0	0
Scheetz	2	0	4
	27	14	68

Rio Grande — Anderson

	G	F	T		G	F	T
Ripperger	2	1	5	Brown	9	9	27
Barr	3	4	10	Lockhart	1	1	3
McKenzie	5	0	10	Renbarger	5	2	12
Wiseman	3	4	10	Ellis	3	2	8
Francis	20	19	59	Kortokrox	6	4	16
Moses	1	1	3	Culp	2	1	5
Gossett	1	2	4	Bartz	0	3	3
				Mofiftt	3	5	11
Totals	35	31	101		29	27	85

Rio Grande — Villanova

	G	F	T		G	F	T
Ripperger	5	6	11	Cirino	3	3	9
Barr	3	0	6	Schafer	11	3	25
Moses	0	0	0	Servon	1	0	2
Francis	16	7	39	Devine	6	4	16
McKenzie	10	5	25	Foley	9	1	19
Wiseman	0	3	3	Tierney	1	2	4
Thompson	1	1	3	Milligan	6	6	18
	35	22	92		37	19	93

Rio Grande	G	F	T	Providence	G	F	T
Wiseman	3	6	12	Moran	9	8	25
McKenzie	3	2	8	Durkin	7	1	15
Francis	13	15	41	Kerr	6	5	17
Barr	4	1	9	McQueney	2	3	7
Ripperger	2	1	5	Reynolds	0	1	1
Moses	2	1	5	Lynch	3	1	7
Thompson	2	4	8	Mullins	5	4	14
Totals	29	30	88		32	23	87

1953-54 ANALYSIS

Record	Won — 21 Lost — 7
Most Team Points	134
Least Team Points	50
Lowest Defensive Total	45
Highest Defensive Total	99
High Point Spread	61
Offensive Average	90.1
Defensive Average	75.7
Attendance	164,000

HIGH GAME TOTALS
CLARENCE "BEVO" FRANCIS

	OPPOSITION	POINTS	SEASON
1.	Ashland Jr. College of KY	116	52-53
2.	Hillsdale College	113	53-54
3.	Alliance College	84	53-54
4.	Bluffton College	82	53-54
5.	Lees College	76	52-53
6.	California State	72	52-53
7.	Wilberforce	69	52-53
8.	Mountain State	66	52-53
9.	Erie Tech.	64	53-54
10.	Mayo State	63	52-53
11.	Lees College	63	52-53
12.	Alliance College	61	53-54
13.	Pikeville College	61	52-53
14.	Mayo State	60	52-53
15.	Anderson College	59	53-54
16.	Sue Bennett	59	52-53
17.	Cincinnati Seminary	59	52-53
18.	Salem College	58	53-54
19.	Wright Patterson Air Force	55	52-53
20.	Ashland College of Ohio	55	53-54

★★★★★★★★★★★★★★★★★★★★★★★★★★★★★★★★

The book, *Incredible Basketball Feats*, by Jim Benagh, published by Grosset and Dunlap of New York, asks the question in the foreword of the book, "What basketball player saved his college from extinction?"

You have just read the answer, according to the author of this book.

COMPILED FROM 1966 N.A.I.A
OFFICIAL RECORD BOOK

NAIA TOP ALL-TIME SINGLE SEASON AVERAGES

Year	Player and School	Games	FG	FT	TTL	AVG.
1953	Bevo Francis, Rio Grande	39	708*	538*	1954*	50.1*
1954	Bevo Francis, Rio Grande	27	460	360	1296	48.0
1964	Willie Shaw, Lane, TN	18	306	121	733	40.7
1965	Thales McReynolds, Miles, AL	18	294	118	706	39.2
1966	Malbert Pradd, Dillard, LA	20	264	253	781	39.0
1963	Bob Johnson, Fitchburg State	17	213	277	703	38.8
1960	Gene Veloff, Doane, NE	11	175	52	402	36.5
1955	George Swyers, WV Tech	18	232	170	634	35.2
1957	Ken Hammond, WV Tech	27	334	274	942	34.9
1956	Bill Reigel, McNeese State	36	425	370	1220	33.9

NAIA INDIVIDUAL SEASON RECORDS

Points	1,954	Bevo Francis, Rio Grande	1953
Field Goals	708	Bevo Francis, Rio Grande	1953
Free Throws	538	Bevo Francis, Rio Grande	1953
Rebounds	738	Gene Hoyt, McKendree, IL	1952

Points, one game 116 Bevo Francis vs. Ashland Kentucky 1953

Consecutive Free Throws made 48, Charlie Horton, Midwester U. Texas 1961

* Denotes record.

NCAA
TOP SINGLE SCORING MARKS

Bevo Francis, Rio Grande	1954	113	Hillsdale College
Frank Selvey, Furman	1954	100	Newberry College
Bevo Francis, Rio Grande	1954	84	Alliance College
Bevo Francis, Rio Grande	1954	82	Bluffton College
Paul Crissman, So. California	1966	80	Pacific Christian
William English, Winston-Salem	1968	77	Fayetteville
Nate DeLong, River Falls State	1948	72	River Falls State
Bevo Francis, Rio Grande	1953	72	California State
Bevo Francis, Rio Grande	1952	69	Wilberforce

ASSOCIATED PRESS CAGE POLL — 1953

New York, February 17, AP: The top collegiate basketball teams in the nation, with points scored on a 109-8-etc. basis. (First place votes in parentheses)

1. Seton Hall (34)
2. Indiana (15)
3. Washington
4. LaSalle (6)
5. Illinois
6. Louisiana State (2)
7. Oklahoma
8. Kansas State
9. Western Kentucky (2)
10. Kansas
11. Seattle (3)
12. Oklahoma City (8)
13. Manhattan
14. De Paul
15. North Carolina S.
16. Louisville (1)
17. Murray KY (2)
18. Duke (1)
19. Villanova
20. Miami
21. Eastern KY
22. Holy Cross
23. Tulsa
24. Fordham
25. Duquesne (1)
26. Rio Grande (1)
27. UCLA
28. Texas

TWO YEAR SUMMARY

Games Played	68	Won-61 Lost-7 Percent-90%	
Team Points	6,519		
Opponents Points	3,913		
Team Average	96.9		
Opponents Average	71.9		
Attendance	244,000		
Largest Attendance Single Game	13,800 (Madison Square Garden)		
Smallest Attendance Single Game	62 (Community Hall)		
Largest Gross Single Game	$34,500.00		
Smallest Gross Single Game	$19.20		

MOST TEAM POINTS ONE GAME
BY RIO GRANDE

1. Ashland Jr. College of KY   150
2. Hillsdale   134
3. Mountain State   133
4. Bluefield   128
5. Ashland College of Ohio   121
6. Erie Tech   120
7. Mayo State   119
8. Ashland College of Ohio   117
9. Alumni   116
10. Salem   115

Coach Newt Oliver and Bevo Francis are seen in hallway of their apartments, which were located next to one another. In Background is Bevo's wife Jean and son Frank, while Newt Oliver's wife Maxine is reading newspaper on right.

BIRTHPLACE OF A LEGEND

In the last 44 years things have changed dramatically in the village of Rio Grande.

The college is now officially known as University of Rio Grande and Rio Grande Community College which is state supported.

It has an enrollment of approximately 2200 and is a fully accredited institution, with many new buildings across the campus, including a modern gymnasium and two auxiliary gyms.

The celebrated gymnasium has been torn down to make way for The Fine and Performing Arts Building.

At the edge of the village, Bob Evans' farm and restaurant stands as a monument to the free-enterprise system and is visited by countless thousands each year.

This is the village of Rio Grande today — 1996.

It has changed in a sensational sort of way in the last 44 years, when it was first rocketed to fame. Then, it seemed to be waiting in quiet expectation for something out-of-the ordinary to happen. Something did.

★★★★★★★★★★★★★★★★★★★★★★★★★★★★★★★★★★★

It happened over 40 years ago in a quiet country village in Southeastern Ohio.

It was planned. But for the ironies of fate, it shouldn't have happened at all.

If Newt Oliver had not returned to Rio Grande College as its coach and athletic director, if Bevo Francis had enrolled at a major college, if Wayne Wiseman had not been one of the greatest ball handlers of all time, if the college had closed its doors forever in 1952.

If, if, if . . .

The odds were infinity-to-one, but at the opportune, now-or-never moment, fate found a new delight. From the odds and ends of chance was to come the most colorful, beloved small college combination in American basketball history.

Rio Grande College has evolved into a modern school now known as the University of Rio Grande, which is pictured above.

Noted Quotes

The production has become too big. Too big even for Oliver, whose blood pressure does strange things when Newt becomes excited or upset.

He is on the spot, and no one realizes it more than himself. It's too late to turn back for the curtain is going up with millions of people in the audience. Will it be an American Success Story or American Tragedy?

Only Father Time has the answer.

Ernie Enfield, Wooster, Ohio Daily
Newspaper
Spring of 1953

No, I'm not actually bitter. But it is hard to be grateful. I guess it was just a case of me getting too many headlines and the president getting too few.

Bevo Francis
Spring of 1954

Bevo Francis is the best pure shooter I have ever seen.

Mel Riebe
The National Basketball
League Scoring Champion 1954
(Fore-runner of the NBA)

To ask you to believe the story of Bevo Francis is to expect you to accept a story that is much like a fairy tale. Even Hollywood does not produce fiction that is so unbelievable.

Guinness - 1980

128

I have seen pressure applied to get teams in to N.I.T. but this time it is not to get a team in, but specifically to keep Rio Grande and Bevo Francis out.

Milton Gross
New York Post Newspaper
March, 1953

Francis is likely to be the only cager in history who gets a bigger roar out of the crowd when he misses than when he connects.

Thad Gardner
Birmingham Post Herald
Newspaper - 1953

Bevo can do things as a Freshman Walter Dukes (All American of Seton Hall) can't do as a senior.

Honey Russell, Coach
Seton Hall University 1953

I am convinced that we are seeing in Bevo the most remarkable publicity build up that I have ever known in all the years that I am acquainted with sports. Don't get me wrong, I love Bevo. But Bevo without an astute coach and publicity man named Newt Oliver would be just an agate line in a box score of a little school in Rio Grande, Ohio.

Al Helfer
"Sports Voice" of Mutual Broadcasting System
Real Magazine - 1953

The big kid from Wellsville, the most amazing youngster since Bob Feller to come down the pike, sank 54 points as Rio Grande College smashed the old Cleveland Arena scoring record in beating Wilberforce University.

Shel Fullerton
Cleveland News
March 1953

Rio Grande College will never be the same since the advent of Bevo Francis and Newt Oliver.

John Short
Marion Star, Marion, Ohio, 1953

Wherever he coached, his teams showed the result of that extra work and energy which is the trademark of the really good coach. Guernsey County and Byesville will hear more— much more—from Newt Oliver, the guy who made good because he refused to fail.

Don Robertson
Byesville Enterprise Newspaper
Byesville, Ohio, 1954

Bevo Francis isn't paying the price of greatness; Coach Newt Oliver is paying it for him.

Earl Flora, Sports Editor
Ohio State Journal - 1953

On Feb. 2, 1954, in Jackson, Ohio, Francis rebuffed the NCAA's snub of the previous year. In a 134-91 victory over Hillsdale College of Michigan, a school that measured up to NCAA standards, Bevo scored 113 points, a single-game scoring record that still stands.

Vince Agul
Los Angeles Times
1986

Beyond the boundaries of Racoon Township, there were few people who could ever correctly pronounce the name of the school—let alone find it, a small dot on the map, 12 miles northeast of Gallipolis on U. S. 35.

Vince Agul
Los Angeles Times
1986

Rio Grande had not won a football game in five years, when they beat Muskingum 7-6 at Wellston, Ohio

Rio Grande College Yearbook 1944

Rio Grande lost to Morehead State of Morehead, Kentucky, 81-15 in basketball.

Rio Grande College Yearbook 1944

Bevo hit his first four shots and matched the entire Butler team through the first two quarters.

Richmond Indiana News Leader Thursday, Jan. 7, 1954

Bevo came, saw and, from all fan reaction, conquered a capacity Gannon Auditorium house last night with an all-time local scoring mark of 61 points that should last until he comes to town again.

Al DeSantis
Erie, Pa. Times
Jan. 1954

Oliver said every field house in which they played was packed and they cheered not only Francis but the whole team, much to the annoyance of the home teams.

Ray Stull, Sports Editor
Jeffersonian Newspaper 1954
Cambridge, Ohio

Selecting the most fascinating personality I've encountered on the sports scene is easy. It is a dual entry named Bevo Francis and Newt Oliver.

Ernie Infield
The Daily Record Newspaper
Wooster, Ohio 1990

Few people qualify as living legends. Newt Oliver is one. On the speaker's stand he is a spellbinder, with an offbeat sense of humor.

Ernie Infield
The Daily Record Newspaper
Wooster, Ohio 1990

The Bevo Francis saga, a rich blend of Americana, comic opera, and sports lore in the best little-guy-makes-good tradition, will add another chapter tonight, this one titled: Rio Grande vs. Butler University.

Angelo Angelopolous
Indianapolis News, Jan. 6, 1954

Ever since coach Newt Oliver and his Bevo brigade piled up Wake Forest and Butler early in the campaign, several authors have been desperately searching for a condiment that will make words edible.

Earl Flora, Sports Editor
Ohio State Journal, 1954

Rio Grande worked out on the Coliseum floor last night and somebody told me this morning Bevo hit 12 consecutive one-handed jump shots from around the foul circle.

Jack Horner, Sports Writer
Raleigh, North Carolina, 1953

The days of the white basketball are gone. That was the trademark of Bevo Francis. It was a special warm-up ball used exclusively by Francis and Oliver often claimed it was the only one of its kind.

In essence with the white ball went Rio Grande's white elephant.

Jack Gilbert, Sports Editor
Athens Messenger
Athens, Ohio, 1956

"I find it hard to believe, after all these years, that it really happened," Newt Oliver, the Redmen's coach reflected a few years ago. Sometimes I wonder if it ever happened at all. It seems like pure fiction.

U.R.G. Newsletter
Oct. 1992

Together, in three short months, they've made the entire nation sit up and take notice of the three-ring basketball show at Rio Grande College.

The little fellow who gets the show on the road is Newt Oliver, a sawed-off, hot-tempered coach in his first year in the college ranks. He's aged 29.

Daves Diles
Associated Pres - 1953

Bliss College recruited me and other players right off the Ohio State campus where I was a student, to play against Rio Grande. We were humiliated 101 to 53.

Dave Dillahunt
Advest stockbroker - 1994
Springfield, Ohio

Experiencing the thrill of watching the graceful Bevo Francis, undoubtedly we fall into the category of those peasants Ohio State Court Coach Floyd Stahl holds in contempt when he described Francis as "sort of the common man's All-American."

Homer Alley
Gallipolis Tribune
November 4, 1953

It shouldn't be necessary to record Bevo's two years of basketball at Rio Grande College in Ohio. Today, he's as famous as the hot dog and even the smallest children know him as the "man who scores 50 points a game."

Jim Obert
The Peoria Star
Feb. 12, 1954

The immediate ambition of Clarence "Bevo" Francis is to score 80 or a 100 points against the University of Miami Hurricanes Saturday night.

Ralph Warner
Miami Daily News
Dec. 1953

No matter where you go these days—at home or abroad—there are two things certain to be in the news; a water shortage and Bevo Francis.

Carl Ebright
Tucker's Town, Bermuda, 1954

Oliver stated, "We pulled off something nobody ever did before." It will never be repeated. How could that ever happen again? I had a major college basketball team in a school with 92 students beating Providence and Wake Forest! And we saved the school!

William Nack
Sports Illustrated Classic
Fall 1992

Oliver seized on Bevo Francis as the means to make the school, and perhaps himself, famous.

Illustrated History of Basketball
By Larry Fox
Grosset and Dunlap, Publishers

Looking back no one can argue that his short, turbulent coaching tenure is the largest single reason the college exists today.

Larry Donald, Editor
Basketball Times, Dec. 31, 1987

The amazing thing is that the Waterloo Wonders basketball team, considered the greatest high school basketball team in history with its two year 97-3 record, and the Redmen of Rio Grande College, were separated in history by 18 years and 18 miles of country roads.

Dave Diles
Associated Press - 1954

The legendary teams Fortieth Reunion, November 1992, in Rio Grande, Ohio. Front Row—Lee Weiher, Jim McKenzie, Coach Newt Oliver, John Viscoglosi, Wayne Wiseman, Roy Moses. Back Row—Dick Myers, Dick Barr, Bevo Francis, Don Vynalek.

135

Fortieth Reunion, November 1992, Rio Grande, Ohio
Left to Right: Bevo Francis, Newt Oliver and Don Vynalek, who later
made "Little All American" at Doane College in Crete, Nebraska

ACKNOWLEDGEMENT

To Hollywood Picture Corporation, a subsidiary of Walt Disney Motion Pictures Group, a special Thanks for buying my "life story rights" for a projected full-length movie.

To Dr. Barry Dorsey, present President of the University of Rio Grande, a sincere Thank You for his encouragement in relating our story in a factual book, which will preserve our legacy in basketball history.

And to Dr. Clyde Evans, Athletic Director of the University of Rio Grande, a sincere and grateful appreciation for his encouragement and direction in helping with the content and structure of this book.

And, last but not least, a special tribute to Coach John Lawhorn, who during his tenure at Rio Grande, has always shown such a respect and dedication toward our program as to earn our on-going and deep appreciation and regard.

In Recognition

Coach, John Lawhorn, who since 1980, has returned the college to a place of prominence among American College Division Mens Teams.

With 33 years of basketball coaching, his combined high school and college record stands at 648 wins and 232 loses.

In 16 years at Rio Grande, his record stands at 375 won and 133 lost, while taking the school to the National NAIA Tournament four times and being named NAIA District Coach of the Year in 1985, 1987, 1991, 1994, and 1995.

In 1975, while coaching at Circleville High School, he was selected "AA" Ohio Associated Press Coach of the Year. In 1980 while coaching at Warren Western Reserve, he was named Ohio's "AAA" Coach of the Year.

Dr. Danny Fulks

Danny Fulks was born in Gallia County, Ohio, near the river village of Crown City, where he graduated from Mercerville High School. He now lives in Huntington, West Virginia. He has a B.S. degree from Rio Grande College, a Masters of Arts degree from Marshall University, and a doctorate from the University of Tennessee. He is a veteran of the U.S. Air Force, and has worked as a grocery store clerk, school bus driver, gasoline attendant, truck driver, gas meter reader, aircraft mechanic, farm laborer, public school teacher, elementary school principal, and college professor. Fulks is veteran faculty member at Marshall University, Huntington, West Virginia, where he teaches writing in the Honor Program. He is the author of four books in the field of education. His articles and essays on Appalachian life have appeared in *Timeline* (Ohio Historical Society), *Hearthstone, Country America, In Buckeye Country, Goldenseal, Now and Then, The Dayton Herald Sunday Magazine,* and *The Columbus Dispatch.* "Fulks heritage is his passport to the region's sometimes impregnable secrets; he knows Appalachia firsthand and travels unimpeded along its highways and byways...By combining accurate description with a peek at the minds and souls of the people he chronicles, Fulks provides a full and breathing account." Christopher S. Duckworth, Editor *Timeline.*